GENERATING HOPE

STORIES OF THE BEAUSOLEIL LOUISIANA SOLAR HOME

W. GEOFF GJERTSON, AIA

& DEGE LEGG

UNIVERSITY OF LOUISIANA AT LAFAYETTE PRESS

University of Louisiana at Lafayette Press
P.O. Box 40831
Lafayette, LA 70504-0831
http://ulpress.org

ISBN 13 (hardcover): 978-1-935754-50-3

Library of Congress Cataloging-in-Publication Data:

Gjertson, W. Geoff, 1967-
Generating Hope : Stories of the BeauSoleil Louisiana Solar Home / by W. Geoff Gjertson, AIA & Dege Legg.
pages cm
"May 7, 2014."
Includes bibliographical references and index.
ISBN 978-1-935754-50-3 (acid-free paper)
1. Solar houses--Louisiana--Design and construction. I. Legg, Dege. II. Title.
TH7414.G54 2014
690'.83704724--dc23
2014018295

Designed by Megan Barra
BeauSoleilHome.org
ULbuildinginstitute.com

PRINTED IN CANADA.

For Alex & Elise

Contents

Portraits

Be Like Beausoleil

Sunrise

Geoff Gjertson

THE BEAUSOLEIL LOUISIANA SOLAR HOME IS THE University of Louisiana at Lafayette's prototypical home created for the Department of Energy's 2009 Solar Decathlon. "BeauSoleil" (pronounced "bo-so-lay") is French for "beautiful sun" (although in Cajun French it generally just means "sunshine.")[1] The Solar Decathlon is an international competition in which twenty select universities design, build, and transport a small 800-square-foot solar-powered home to the National Mall in Washington, D.C. For two weeks, they compete in ten different contests that evaluate the livability and performance of the homes.[2] The BeauSoleil Home won one of the ten contests - Market Viability - which meant that is was the most livable, constructible, and marketable among the international competition. It was also selected by over 17,000 votes as the People's Choice Winner.[3]

But the BeauSoleil Louisiana Solar Home is so much more than just a science fair winner. Although it was created for the Solar Decathlon, it was never simply about winning a competition. The home embodies the hearts, souls, ingenuity, way of life, and spirit of the Cajun[4] and Creole[5] people of South Louisiana. The BeauSoleil Home captures the past and present. And it represents a possible future direction for energy-efficient and hurricane-resistant housing on the Gulf Coast.

Like the *frottoir* (washboard used in Zydeco music) the BeauSoleil Home is not extravagant or over-wrought. It is simple and modest. The BeauSoleil Home is first and foremost functional. Just as Cajun and Creole culture has traditionally done, it makes the most of a little. Social interaction, in the form of entertaining and cooking, are the daily rituals that inspire its form. The home adapts to the unexpected, whether it be a spontaneous visitor, an unplanned crawfish boil, or a hurricane.

This book is the story of the BeauSoleil Home. It is a story of a dedicated core team of University of Louisiana at Lafayette student officers, over 200 other university students, and a handful of university professors working with construction professionals for over two years to design and build a solar home. And these are the stories of the entire University, community, and state investing their finances and dreams to fuel this ambitious mission.

What was the return on this investment of creativity, blood, sweat, tears, and resources? For the students, it was an experience that continues to guide them in their careers as architects, engineers, and other professionals. For the professors, the home has been a source of applied research and teaching for new generations of students. And for everyone - including those who visit the home today for the first time - the BeauSoleil Louisiana Solar Home has the ability to generate hope.

BELOW

Home at Sunrise in D.C.

How Solar Decathlons Can Alter Design Education, Our Profession, and Our Communities

Pliny Fisk III

GEOFF AND EDDIE KNOW HOW MUCH I LOVE THIS project and I appreciate being asked to contribute in some way to this wonderful story of how technology and culture can come together to create a significant model for the way we teach and practice architecture. Seldom in a university setting are architecture students or faculty placed in a position where they actually might fail and learn from it. At best we design-build a cool bus stop, vegetable stand, or (if we are lucky) a single affordable house – nothing nearly as complex socially or technically advanced as a Solar Decathlon home.

The extremely unique tiny home competition crisscrosses several significant issues facing not only the manner in which we deliver buildings but how we design/engineer and test them as technical as well as societal performers. In my experience as an adviser to several Decathlon homes, the following strategies stood out:

1. The ability to resolve technical complexity through systems-thinking yet remain, above all good designers.
2. Jumping out of university walls and developing partnerships with experienced community-based, culturally and technically-savvy non-profits.
3. Creating a T.R.Y. – "try-it-yourself" mentality before using the public as an experiment.
4. Discovering new construction systems adapted from off-the-shelf components.

An important part of the Solar Decathlon experience is to become part of a social/economic infrastructure where units of production and consumption are understood and developed at the community level – and by so doing, help build broad relationships in what some call a civic ecology. Design education must go through this systems-thinking transformation that is ecological in the broadest sense. Solar Decathlons, in general, and the experiences I am about to highlight from UT Austin and Texas A & M, represent an important history of this educational transition. It is quite a different experience from what was done at my favorite Solar Decathlon home of them all – the BeauSoleil Louisiana Solar Home from UL Lafayette.

My organization, the Center for Maximum Potential Building Systems, believes in an Eco-systems approach – maximizing potential is an inbuilt striving mechanism to always attain the next point in our evolutionary process. Since we are now this country's oldest continuously operating non-profit sustainable architecture and planning office, we feel that our thinking processes are as critical as the result we provide, and we will now and then refer to what has become our "lenses" for creating maximum potential future methodologies gleaned from almost 40 years of a hard knocks building system experience.[1]

ABOVE
Texas A & M 2007 Solar Decathlon House

I am an over-educated refugee from perhaps the best architecture and planning school in the United States at the time, the University of Pennsylvania in the late '60s. I was intimately connected to those who were considered the best of the best – Louis Kahn, Robert Venturi, Le Ricolais, Ian McHarg, and Russell Ackoff. I came out of graduate school so totally spoiled that if I had not, by some fate, come to Texas, I would have been a career professional similar (if I were so lucky) to some of my academic peers (Renzo Piano, Susan Maxman, or Charlie Doggett). But immediately after graduation I was fortunate to be asked to join Ian McHarg's office, and my ex-wife Daria Bolton did the same with Louis Kahn's office. We became highly immersed in two of the greatest architecture and ecological planning offices in the country. Even though we were having success, we decided to go in a direction that some would call back words – i.e., start in the trenches from bottom up, not top down. We decided for some unknown reason to spread our wings and go, to of all places, the University of Texas at Austin. I had no idea that I was about to enter a realm where the clashes of culture, income, border issues, and conservative politics were at its pinnacle and that I was squarely in the middle of a successful good old boy, oil-financed state that pushed "the haves and have-nots" even further apart.

We immediately placed our students into our own type of university "skunk works" (The Center for Maximum Potential Building Systems) so they could experience firsthand what a sustainable building or lifestyle was about before telling others. The real question was: could we work with the most basic conditions and really test ourselves as viable global citizens? Would we professional educators and students have the capacity to learn an entirely new set of skills so we could become valuable designers for the majority of the people in Texas and elsewhere? Soon I was working in Central America, Indian nations, and other places asking about the changes that we all would have to make. That was about the time that I briefly joined forces with some of the early activists in rural Louisiana that Eddie Cazayoux mentions in his Foreword – the Buck Nellis crowd, as I called them, including radical priests like Father Bill and other down and dirty people in the trenches all over the South Coast from Brownsville to New Orleans.

As time went on, I found that my previous faculty "friends" at UT would no longer let their students even visit our non-profit (because we were working with radicals, I was told.) I soon learned to leverage field work and used the publicity that I was receiving from NPR, the *New York Times*, and the *Christian Science Monitor*, to bridge into the policy arena. After being invited to testify to sub-committees of the House and the Senate, I became part of a team that created such institutions as the National Center for Appropriate Technology and eventually the American Institute of Architect's Committee on the Environment – some of the only programs that understood and supported these efforts. Gradually this created other opportunities, including national and international awards. Now I was sought after by the very university that had questioned our work, and they hired me to accomplish what they had little skill or resources to pull off – an off-the-grid, quickly deployable-building system for the Solar Decathlon competition.

UT was the first. I, and CMPBS, ended up as major players in creating the UT project for the cost of a visiting summer faculty salary – that included all our facilities (metal and wood working shops) and my entire staff. This was a totally unexpected relationship especially since we were dealing with one of the wealthiest universities in the country

My knowledge of Texas's rural south came into play. I pointed out to the students the mobile home culture that was dominant in most rural areas and soon convinced them to use a mobile home as the core of the home in conjunction with a

Dogtrot approach to ventilation. I pushed for the building to use protocols for assembly and disassembly. I pushed even harder for the use of some simple innovations like a system for assembly and disassembly based on our work creating the first State Demonstration Farm. At that farm, I wisely used recycled drilling stems from oil rigs to support all the shade and building structures and raise the roofs of barn-type buildings. This simple means of construction was enthusiastically received by both farmers and ranchers.

BELOW
State Demonstration Farm, Laredo, TX

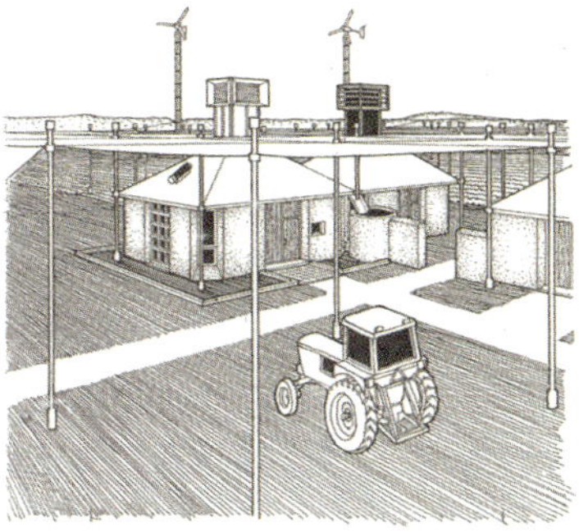

So why could we not place our shed roof of the Solar Decathlon home on the ground, slide the solar PV's onto the roof while still on the ground, as we had with the Demonstration Farm, and hoist everything up at once? When UT faculty came to get a peek at what was going on, they were appalled. Nothing was done in any traditional manner. To get the building aesthetics up to speed I pushed for the use of an Airstream as the mobile home so we were not perceived as Texas Hillbillies. Again criticism - what did an Airstream have to do with a Solar Decathlon home on the Mall? The reality was it might have been the first-ever, properly-insulated Airstream in the United States - a model in of itself. So to Washington we went, maybe a bit unprepared (i.e., not enough preassembled electrical harnesses or preassembled plumbing and an unworkable ice battery), but we made it. Our most prestigious award came in the form of Third Place in Design, which was pushed by Jurors Steve Badanes and Glenn Murcutt who loved the construction, climatic, and Airstream aspects. But the most amazing part of the entire process was the extreme criticism coming from UT for being over budget at $168K - not winning enough awards and being apparently critical of their prize student who had created a large amount of waste in the fabrication process.

Little did I know it at the time, but one of the most significant things that happened on the Mall in 2002 was that Texas A & M's team was asked to leave and return to College Station

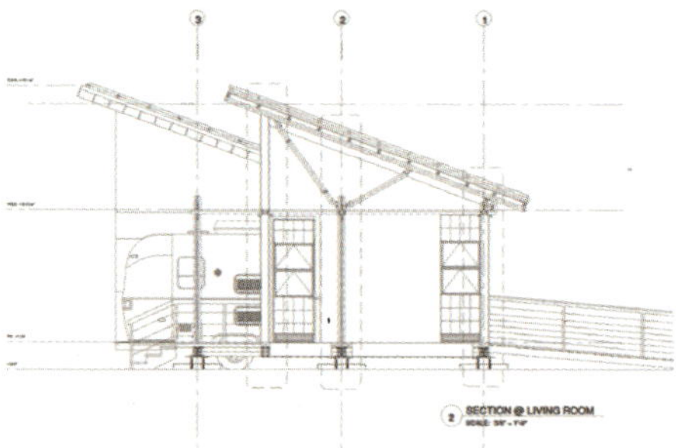

TOP
UT Austin 2002 Solar Decathlon House

OPPOSITE TOP
Texas A & M 2007 Solar Decathlon House

OPPOSITE MIDDLE RIGHT
Texas A & M 2007 Solar Decathlon House Fatwall Construction

OPPOSITE BOTTOM
Interior Texas A & M 2007 Solar Decathlon House

because they could not finish their building in time. An entire entourage soon came to CMPBS to offer me a tenured faculty position and a $750,000 production facility. So back and forth from Austin to College Station I went for 6 years resulting in an untold number of speeding tickets! From the start, A & M was a very different place than I was used to with across-the-board administrative and faculty support and students from at least three departments on the team.

Then significant events took place in 2005 – Katrina hit in August then Rita in September and Texas and the Gulf Coast were devastated. I wondered how a Solar Decathlon could make not only a statement about these events but perhaps even become a solution – i.e., produce hurricane worthy homes. So in addition to the ten tests of the Decathlon, we added our own criteria, including:

1. Design for Reuse (DfRU – a CMPBS Lens): Incorporating mothballed FEMA trailer frames as the structural components to create wind-resistant homes.
2. Design for Evidence-Based Economics (DfEBE – a CMPBS Lens): Responding to typical middle-class families' economic needs by creating solutions in building terms (such as a "growable core base" to pay off loans gradually, a revenue-producing vehicle-to-grid garage, and a living-machine, insect-fed guano garden to reduce health risks from yard toxins such as fertilizers and insecticides.)
3. Plan at a community mixed-use level: Using a stackable core building – not just a single home, in order to create an economics of scale and advantages of community solar infrastructure.
4. Encourage a sustainable life style (ecoBalance[2] – a CMPBS's Lens): Completing life cycles from source to resource, and Visible Green (designing iconographic reminders of cyclical routines.)
5. Design for Manufacturing (DfM – a CMPBS lens): A system that worked on the factory floor including plug and play fat-walls attached to the main frame to create a parallel production sequence.

So we set the bar high and, in the end, we received many awards.[3] And the administration, for the most part, was overjoyed. But the most important result was how the

younger generation learned a bevy of valuable thinking, doing, and people-skills. They also learned management, including critical path methodology, and an introduction to gaming as a process for enabling users to understand building systems and community. Technically, the experience fit squarely into the middle of what are now called the Maker, Gaming, and Biophilic movements. Additionally, some students moved on to careers in the building system production arena.

So at CMPBS, the non-profit trouble makers on the east side of Austin, where all the cultural creatives live, work, and play every day - there are two Solar Decathlon homes - one UT and the other A & M, which have been open to over 100 public tours in the last 7-1/2 years.

---

[1] Lenses for a Maximum Potential Future: Visible Green; ProtoScope; EcoBalance; Supports & Connections; Gamification; Area Point Network; Green Health; Baseline Green/GreenBalance; Feedback City; Mini Max; Meta Max; Conceptual Space Race. See all Lenses on CMPBS website: http://cmpbs.org/what-we-do/tool-development.

[2] See EcoBalance on the CMPBS website: http://cmpbs.org/projects/2000/ecobalance?tid=17.

[3] 2007 Texas A&M Solar Decathlon awards and recognition: 1st Place: Appliance Category, Department of Energy; 1st Place: AIA Student Choice Award; 1st Place: Student building category, EPA LifeCycle Building Challenge; 3rd Place: Curb Appeal, National Association of Home Builders; Featured on Sundance Channel "Big Ideas for a Small World" Only entry featured out of 20 total entries.

Foreword

Edward J. Cazayoux, FAIA

As I PREPARED FOR RETIREMENT FROM THE University, I bonded with Geoff Gjertson who, like me, was interested in hands-on learning for students. Geoff was a person who liked to build things and had the tools and skills to do so. Hector LaSala and I, along with the faculty in the 1980s, had developed an architectural curriculum for the University of Louisiana at Lafayette School of Architecture & Design based on hands-on work that stimulated the creative spirit. We understood the advantage of having the students use information that was presented to them and building things that turned information into knowledge. We perceived that there was a direct link between your hands and right brain creative thinking. Even when computers started to be integrated into the curriculum, we kept the students building and drawing for the first year and a half before they could use a computer. That is how important we felt the hands-on activity/experience was to a creative education. I also think it is important for architects to be able to build their designs and not just visualize them. If this were always so, we would have much better architecture.

After I retired from the University, Geoff contacted me about the Solar Decathlon. I encouraged him to go for it. I helped with the nomination package and was thrilled when they got the invitation to participate. Geoff is a persistent hard-working professor who pushed for an excellent proposal. How excited I was for Geoff and the students who would be working on this project.

After he had assembled the TEAM, I took them to Pointe Coupee Parish, a very early French settlement, to see and experience 18th and 19th-century French colonial architecture around False River – an architecture developed by the colonists to be comfortable in our hot and humid climate. The architecture they first built was very inappropriate because their ancestors had developed it for a colder climate in France. Their architecture in South Louisiana went through a climatic adaptation from the mother country's rural areas in Normandy, Brittany, and Calvados to produce an architecture that acclimated to this new place. This trip with the students was a good grounding in the basics. What did our ancestors do to be comfortable without the technology we have today? This type of study provides great insight as to what is appropriate for this area. Shading and ventilation were the predominant elements of comfort. Structures were picked up off the ground, porches were added around the exterior, the interior ceiling was raised, and more openings were provided. The colonists adapted their architecture to this new climate.

ABOVE
Jacques Dupré Home, Pointe Coupee Parish, LA

Another good grounding was introduced through a group that Elemore Morgan Jr. and I pulled together of older people who lived close to the land without electricity, running water, or municipal sewage treatment. There was also one young energetic person – Tony Adrian, whom I had designed an off-the-grid sustainable house for a few years back. These basic living conditions are the essence of passive design. And for sustainable design, you incorporate as many passive elements into the design to keep the energy requirements to a minimum. The students learned about collecting rainwater for the important things like making your coffee, washing your hair and finer clothes, drinking and cooking with. And you used bayou or well water to clean the house, wash the dishes, and clean fish. Providing food was a seasonal way of life – growing, hunting, and fishing for your food. Rooms in the house were multi-purpose from day to night. The porch was a social space that connected you to the community and the natural environment, and probably was the most used space of the house. It was easy for the students to relate to this because it was part of their culture.

I was impressed that the students wanted the design of the home to reflect the culture of South Louisiana. Even though the Solar Decathlon rules and regulations seemed designed to develop a generic house, the students said it needed to be a home for Louisiana, a design we could bring back and

RIGHT

Sun Relief at Cazayoux Home

reproduce as affordable housing for the people of this area - an abode that relates to and ties residents to the local natural environment. We, as human beings, developed with a very close relationship to the environment. Our whole soul and psyche are closely tied to the natural environment. And architecture is one of the major resources that can be designed to help tie you back to the environment. Not only are environmentally responsive buildings more sustainable, they also provide a stage for occupants to dance to the rhythms of the changing seasons, a dance that brings mankind a little closer to the wonders of the natural world - a dance and relationship that makes your life much richer.

The students imagined a home that was functional, local - of South Louisiana, self-sufficient and beautiful (*beau*). They are remarkable individuals. This competition is a powerful reminder that self-sufficiency is plausible and worth working towards. In addition, an architecture that relates to the people and the place was absolutely necessary. The TEAM insisted that the design be basic, simple, and straightforward. And it was beautiful!

I invited two architects who had inspired me to visit and talk with the students. Pliny Fisk III, co-director of the Center for Maximum Potential Building Systems (which he started in Austin, Texas, in 1975) and who had worked with the University of Texas and Texas A&M to do their Solar Decathlon projects a few years earlier, was the first guest. Pliny had come to Lafayette to work with a group of us in the 1980s, including Hector LaSala, (who was interested in solar energy) and our organization named Shine On Louisiana Acadiana Region (S.O.L.A.R.) with Bucky Nellis and Father Bill. Pliny was a big help in showing us how to help people reduce their energy needs with simple methods of better housing. Pliny was also very helpful in pointing out the stumbling blocks of the Decathlon competition. The other guest I invited was Edward Mazria, a fellow of the American Institute of Architects, who I had known through the American Solar Energy Society from the early 1970s. In the late 1970s, Ed wrote THE book, *The Passive Solar Energy Book,* which was the bible for any of us working in the field. An award winning architect, Ed gave up his practice in 2003 to start "The 2030 Challenge" which is a charge to architects to reduce our carbon footprint to zero by that date. Ed was also one of the judges for one of the previous Solar Decathlons. Ed is an energy motivational speaker who filled the Angelle Auditorium on the UL Lafayette campus with students, faculty, and many of Lafayette's leaders. He stayed on to meet with the students and critique their work on the Solar Decathlon project.

Geoff and the students did an incredible job of raising the funding to do such a project and carrying through with the design and construction of the house. It was done on a shoestring. Some other projects cost millions of dollars. Geoff kept the cash spent to $400,000 and the in-kind materials/services to $400,000. This is incredible due to the fact that the structure had to be built here, disassembled and shipped to Washington, erected on the Mall, disassembled and brought back to the University, and reassembled. What a marathon project for anyone.

As I had done when building the Cade Research House, which was also a U.S. Department of Energy funded project, with students in the early 1980s, Geoff did not always follow protocol when push came to shove, and he was reprimanded for his actions. But sometimes that has to happen to get things done, and building a house with students is not something with a handbook to follow. The important thing is that the work got done. As they say, "Sometimes it is better to be fussed at than to ask permission and be denied." Sometimes you just have to do what you have to do to get things done.

The biggest *faux pas* of the project was my suggestion that the water heater be a multipurpose machine. We could have just purchased a solar water heater and have been done with it, but nooooo... My little mind told me that we could get extra credit for innovation on this one. I had built flat plate solar collectors to heat water when I was living in Colorado, but this would be much more. The idea was to have operable fins that water could run through. Right there someone should have said running water through movable parts is not a good idea. One side of the fin would be painted flat black and the other side white. This would have been installed over the multipurpose porch or the Dogtrot part of the house. This collector would be able to produce hot water during the day and cool water during the night. It would also act as a shading device to keep the sun out of that space or reflect more daylight in. I worked with Don Begneaud of Begneaud Manufacturing to develop such a fin, but I did not follow through with the entire system. I think the truth is that it was put off for too long to get developed and ended up as a fixed fin solar water heater only. Experimentation and prototyping have to be given the time for things to evolve, for mistakes to be made, and improvements to be developed.

While our students were systematically working very hard to put BeauSoleil together, some other universities had hired construction crews to do this work and finish it. This did not seem fair. The regulations also did not seem fair that we could not put a roofed porch on our house. After all, South Louisiana's culture and climate were the students' driving force behind their design. This was probably the most impressive aspect on the project – the students demanded that if they got one of the 20 nominations what they would bring to the Mall was a house of and for South Louisiana. The design criteria and regulations were generic, but the house responded to the people and climate back home. They stuck to their main design criteria and it paid off.

And this was not missed by the visitors on the Mall or the judges. Some houses had a microwave and a dishwasher for a kitchen. Our students understood that the kitchen is a social and cooking stage for the family and friends that visit. Cooking and the *joie de vivre* of food is the heart of a South Louisiana house and a cultural ritual. Life is a ritual. The home you live in should aid you in this celebration of life. BeauSoleil was designed like a sailboat – when the wind is blowing you raise the sails to move with the energy of nature. Riding on the wind is magical. Sustainable architecture is equally magical and profound. It helps tie you to the natural environment.

On the last day for public visitation and review of the houses on the Mall, it was cold and rainy so I hung out in the kitchen after visiting all the other houses to see how many were leaking. The comment I heard from one after another of the visitors coming through was "oh – I could live here." This was probably the first house that they saw that had a usable kitchen. BeauSoleil was much more than another house on display at the Mall, it was a home. And that is what won it first place in the Market Viability category and the People's Choice Award. It was a success.

To Geoff and the TEAM, I say congratulations. You did way more than design and build a house. You built a tight knit community of individuals and you raised yourself much higher than any course in the curriculum. I want all of you to know how proud I am of you, and how happy I am that you asked me to be part of the TEAM.

BELOW

Eddie and Faye Cazayoux in the Dogtrot in D.C.

Introduction

IT IS A LIFE-CHANGING EXPERIENCE. Designing, building, and transferring the technology of the BeauSoleil Louisiana Solar Home was probably a once in a lifetime opportunity for the University of Louisiana at Lafayette and the community to embark on a multifaceted journey into the realm of sustainable housing on a national stage.[6] As I write this introduction, I am flying to Washington, D.C., for Easter break with my family. Washington is where five years ago we competed in the 2009 Solar Decathlon, which was the initial impetus for the design and construction of the BeauSoleil Home. The project felt like a decade of work wrapped in two years. When I started thinking about writing a book about the BeauSoleil Home, it was primarily out of obligations to things that were bigger than me: the TEAM, our University, our community, and the home itself. So many people gave their all to make the home a reality that the journey deserved to be documented.

Over the last two years, the book has begun to embody many other things as well.[7] It has been cathartic to reflect on the monumental endeavor of the BeauSoleil Home - the time, the planning, the ideas, and the number of people involved. The project exacted a toll on many of them, and it is a toll that I hope has brought many rewards for all the participants. Often the reflective part of any work is as important as the actual work itself.[8] And unfortunately, too often we bypass this opportunity for insight. Finally, uncovering all these issues intertwined with the drama of the project I hope will draw in readers. As my editor/co-writer Dege Legg says, "This is a victory lap."[9] We accomplished what we set out to do: designing and building a culturally and regionally appropriate, hybrid of active and passive systems, that can eventually become a prototype for an affordable (to the median-income family) and sustainable home.[10] This was proven because out of 20 of the best university designed homes in the world, ours was judged by the jury "First Place" in

Market Viability (livability, buildability, and marketability.)[11] That was our goal: to build a better home for our people.

Three narratives structure the book. First, there is a chronological narrative of the two plus years of the project and its later influences. I believe it is a compelling story of planning, execution, and even some serendipity. Next, the book provides valuable and readily implementable sustainable home design strategies that were employed in the BeauSoleil Home. And unlike Google, which gives generic FAQ's, we strive for specificity and honesty in the things that worked well and the things that didn't work so well. Finally, and most importantly, this book tells the stories of the PEOPLE of the BeauSoleil Home: the TEAM that designed and built the home and the PARTNERS in the University and community that supported the effort.

That brings me to the title of the book, *Generating Hope*. As I examined, researched, and pondered the project and its significance, I realized that the most lasting and salient feature of the entire experience was HOPE.[12] Hope was one of the primary motivations for tackling the project and one of its greatest by-products. After all, the BeauSoleil Home was never really about itself or the Solar Decathlon competition. After five years and hundreds of thousands of hours, what really matters are the people affected and their hopes for the future.

THE STORIES

tastes and smells of
home. As time passes
the sun comes around
face the home, you
create a suitable
wardrobe for the day
enhancing her inner
atmosphere.

Motivations

WHY WOULD OVER 200 PEOPLE SPEND TWO years designing and building a single solar home? The reasons are many and quite varied. For some it was the competitive aspect of the U.S. Department of Energy's Solar Decathlon. For others it was the determination to design a house that was truly sustainable. After all, sustainability is needed in our world of dwindling resources and sustainable living, or at the least the idea of sustainable living, is somewhat fashionable. (And if it takes "fashion" to have it accepted, so be it.) For me, as the lead faculty adviser for the BeauSoleil Louisiana Solar Home, it was the desire to design and build a house in the biggest arena for design/build education. This desire, combined with the imperative to build and teach sustainably, made the 2009 Solar Decathlon a mandate.

The Solar Decathlon is a competition sponsored by the Department of Energy. Every two years, 20 universities from

around the country and world are selected to design, build, and transport a solar-powered house to Washington, D.C., and compete in 10 contests that rate performance and livability. This book is the story of the two-year journey to the competition, the event itself, and finally, the subsequent impact on the University of Louisiana at Lafayette, our community, and the Gulf Coast region. As is true with most trips, the path taken and the trials and tribulations along the way are as important as the destination, if not more.

ABOVE
Past Solar Decathlon

LEFT
New Orleans Shotgun

BELOW
Stuart Woody Guest House, Pointe Coupee Parish, LA

The BeauSoleil Louisiana Solar Home is inextricably connected to the culture of Louisiana and the American South. Its name was borrowed from one of the most famous Cajun bands in Louisiana. Its form evolved from the traditional raised Acadian Cottage, New Orleans Shotgun, and Southern Dogtrot home types.[13] It reflects the *joie de vivre* of entertaining by graciously accommodating the impromptu parties and gatherings that are so much a part of the area's culture.[14] In addition, the BeauSoleil Home is filled with Louisiana art and literature.

Beyond the more obvious references to arts and culture, how is the BeauSoleil Home connected to the culture of our region any more than any other building? I believe it is in the process that gave birth to the home which could be described as inclusive and integrated. The process grew and evolved as we went. Even deciding to do the project was intuitive – it was the right thing to do at the right time.

Our local culture is spontaneous and improvisational. The Acadians who originally moved to our region learned to make-do with what they found, and they continued to put emphasis on their families. They were and continue to be craftspeople. They craft everything, meaning they put great care in whatever they do, be it cooking, carving, sewing, or making music.

Much like their Cajun and Créole ancestors, the students who worked on the BeauSoleil Home chose to work on the project. They were not forced to do the project or hand-picked or even talked into it. The TEAM grew organically. Leaders emerged naturally. And ultimately the design grew. The home took shape from a collaborative effort of precedent analysis and research. There were no individual egos on the project just a TEAM ego.

Geoff Gjertson

LEAD FACULTY ADVISER, PROFESSOR OF ARCHITECTURE, AND ARCHITECT

Lead faculty adviser for TEAM BeauSoleil, Geoff Gjertson was the prime moving force that vigilantly paved the way for the project from beginning to end – an exhausting, but rewarding endeavor he openly cherishes to this day. Born in Huntsville, Alabama, Gjertson grew up in seven different locations across the United States, a transcontinental odyssey dictated by his father's career as a defense contractor. The self-confessed habitual "perfectionist," raised by lifelong overachievers, perpetuated that legacy a little further when he committed himself and UL Lafayette to the BeauSoleil project. Gjertson graduated from Arizona State with his Bachelor's degree and received his Master's of Architecture from Rice University. He became a licensed architect in 1994, and his work has won numerous awards and has been published in several professional and academic journals. In 2001, he and his family settled in Lafayette where the Professor of Architecture had been teaching since 2000.

"Because we moved a lot when I was young, my parents were always looking at homes," says Gjertson. "Both of them were very into modern architecture and a lot of unique designs. So that's how I got interested in architecture. For about 10 years, I worked for various architecture firms and had gotten to a point where I was licensed and on track to become a partner in a firm. But I didn't want that, because it took me further away from what I liked about architecture, which was doing the actual work and designing.

"If you're going to do anything good, you're going to do more than the minimum requirements, and that's what the students involved in this project did. It was about something bigger. From start to finish, over 200 students were involved in BeauSoleil. We had a very open, collaborative process. Everyone was very willing to let it become what it would become. It was an opportunity that one seldom gets, which is to design and build something the way you really think it should be designed. Although, they were limited by some rules of the contest, they could really dream and incorporate materials and systems that they normally would not be able to.

HOPE:
"There's two parts to hope: one is what you want in the future, and the other is what you need for your well being. Hope is happiness."

"A lot of people think that the BeauSoleil Home is my house or my design. It's not. I wasn't the designer. It was the students. To use a football analogy, I functioned more like a coach on the sidelines. But I'm not a 'rah!-rah!' kind of guy. I'm competitive, but I'm not about winning at all costs. Winning the competition was not my primary motivation for doing this project. I was more interested in building something unique that people would want to live in and something that represented what Louisiana has to offer. The house is innovative, but it draws upon what was already here in terms of the culture and technology. We didn't invent anything new; we just reassembled it in a new way that was a clear encapsulation of our culture."

The BeauSoleil Home incorporates advanced technology. It is also a no-nonsense response to the pleasures and problems of living on the Gulf Coast. However, many of the home's features are not innovative. They are derivations of what has worked before. What is new and innovative is the distillation of these concepts into one small, lovingly crafted home - a home that captured the hopes and dreams of the TEAM and the community. We put all of our eggs in the BeauSoleil basket, and everyone who worked on it dedicated their lives to it, at least for a while. This is the journey from my point of view intertwined with the stories of my colleagues, students, and partners.

IN MAY OF 2007, MY WIFE GERMAINE AND I ATTENDED the American Institute of Architects' National Convention in San Antonio, Texas. There we heard Al Gore speak. Since the construction industry is the biggest polluter and consumer of resources, he placed a mandate on the architectural profession to reduce our carbon footprint.[15] He also stated that the architectural profession had the greatest opportunity and potential to improve the environment through sustainable design. It was an inspiring speech and one of my initial motivations to pursue sustainable design education at the University of Louisiana at Lafayette. Although the idea of "living with nature" had always been an integral part of our teaching at UL Lafayette, these urgent times required a more focused and immersive approach to the education of our future architects.[16]

To amplify this, my colleague Onezieme Mouton and I attended the Association of Collegiate Schools of Architecture Teachers Conference at the Cranbrook Academy in Detroit in July 2007.[17] The scientist David Orr, from Oberlin College, spoke, and his presentation altered my thinking forever. Professor Orr told the educators, in not so few words, that unless the architectural profession made strides in reducing greenhouse gas, we would all be breathing on respirators after 2050. Germaine and I may be gone by then but our children, Alex and Elise, will be 51 and 54 in 2050, and my grandchildren will probably be in their teens or 20s. The image of this scenario is devastating to me. It was a call to action.

I had been following the Solar Decathlon since it started in 2002. The Decathlon is known as the most intense and noteworthy student design/build competition in the world. Photographs of the Solar Decathlon homes were always prominently featured in the magazines and seeing this inspired me to compete. One of my mentors at the University of Louisiana at Lafayette is Professor Emeritus Edward J. Cazayoux. He is the foremost expert on Louisiana architecture and passive/environmental design *and* one of the wisest, wittiest, and noblest men I know. He suggested a year or two earlier that UL Lafayette participate in the Decathlon. However, at the time, he was retired, and there didn't seem to be anyone else on the faculty interested in the competition. Thus, I knew I would have to spearhead the effort.

I had been teaching at UL Lafayette for seven years when the Solar Decathlon came along. Just four years earlier, under the shared leadership of Dean Gordon Brooks, Professor Cazayoux, Professor Hector LaSala, Director Robert McKinney, and I, the Building Institute, a formalized program of design/build, service-learning had been created. The mission of the Building Institute is to teach design through hands-on making while serving the community and helping to preserve our history and culture.[18] With the help of Cazayoux and students, the Building Institute had completed the disassembly, moving, and historic restoration of an 1850s raised Acadian cottage at the Vermilionville Living History Museum.[19] This project took two years and countless hours to complete. Then working with LaSala and students, the Building Institute had designed and built installations on the campus of the Acadiana Outreach Center, a homeless shelter. These installations were small for the most part, with the largest being an outdoor performance space. Our work was featured in the *New York Times* [20] and *Metropolis Magazine*.[21]

After the Outreach Center, the Building Institute began an initiative with Professor LaSala to help the Boys and Girls Clubs of Acadiana. The institute's students designed and built installations, a playground, and a tensile fabric structure for one of the club's basketball courts. In addition, the Building Institute and the local chapter of the American Institute of Architects expanded the process by holding brainstorming sessions, known as *charrettes*, with the stakeholders at each of the five regional clubs to help master plan future improvements.

Professor Cazayoux and Professor LaSala were instrumental in reinventing the School of Architecture and Design in the 1980s. They introduced a pedagogy that utilized hands-on making and Maria Montessori's ideas of play and exploration

Edward J. Cazayoux

PROFESSOR EMERITUS OF ARCHITECTURE

Born and raised in New Roads, Louisiana, Eddie Cazayoux grew up fishing, boating, and skiing on False River as well as working at his father's cotton gin. A world traveler, Army veteran, a distinguished Fellow of the American Institute of Architects, and a recipient of numerous awards from the U.S. Dept. of Energy, U.S. Dept. of the Interior-National Park Service, AIA Louisiana, and the State of Louisiana-Energy Division, Cazayoux is considered the spiritual godfather of the BeauSoleil Home. His sage advice and prolific knowledge of Louisiana architecture and the sustainable practices used in those homes over hundreds of years provided an invaluable resource for the design and creation of the BeauSoleil Home. These historic designs informed many of the ideas of the BeauSoleil Home, including energy saving techniques and practices that were standard in Louisiana homes 200 years ago.

HOPE:

"Hope is a wish or desire. I have hope for a few things, but for the things that are really important. And I have faith that they will come to fruition. I believe that we are spiritual beings having a physical experience on this earth – a planet that was created for us to live *with* and not just *on*. It is our home and our means of survival. Take care of it and it will take care of us."

"In my architectural education, I realized that architecture is shelter from the natural environment, which is a good thing at times, but it removed you from experiencing the natural world," says Cazayoux. "I wanted to do just the opposite; I saw architecture as an opportunity to help connect people to the natural environment.

"The old Louisiana homes were built before there was electricity. There was a basis of techniques for dealing with the natural environment and with the natural materials that were here. You don't get any more sustainable than that old architecture. They didn't use any energy at all. It's only been in the last 60 years that we've removed ourselves from that with air conditioning and all of that. Our whole soul and psyches are tied to the environment."

into the curriculum.[22] The German architecture and design school the Bauhaus had utilized these teaching techniques as well, wherein students would learn to design and make highly-crafted small objects like candlesticks, before eventually progressing to buildings.[23]

ABOVE
Texas A & M 2007 Solar Decathlon House

In October of 2007, with my colleagues Professors LaSala and Michael McClure, I went to the Association of Collegiate Schools of Architecture Fall Conference at Catholic University in Washington, D.C.[24] While there, we visited the 2007 Solar Decathlon that was underway. We knew instantly that the University of Louisiana at Lafayette's School of Architecture and Design could do better. For one, none of the entries had any soul or cultural personality, except Texas A&M's entry.[25] The houses were for the most part generic, technological wonders that were exorbitantly expensive. Texas A&M's home had a richness and complexity that connected the visitor to the landscape. Its architecture conveyed ideas of craft and culture through materials and forms. Like their regional approach, it became our goal to design a house for Louisiana's culture and climate and to do it affordably.

During the fall 2007 semester, my graduate assistant, Piyaont (Gate) Boonklurb and I began researching the Solar Decathlon. That year I was also the president of the South Louisiana Chapter of the American Institute of Architects, and we were hosting the Louisiana State AIA Conference in Lafayette. I suggested the theme of *RR Crossing: reBuilding Responsibly* and invited Shigeru Ban (the 2014 Pritzker Prize Laureate) to be the keynote speaker.[26] His humanitarian, regionally-responsive, and ecological work was certainly inspiring for all. Ban's quote, "I hate waste," has stayed with me since then.[27] How can three words ever say more succinctly what sustainability is?

In general, the Gulf Coast's economy, including that of Lafayette, is largely built on oil and gas production. The word "solar" is sometimes a threat to many who make their livelihood in the oilfield, carrying with it many pop-cultural associations that don't always mesh with the hardworking, conservative instincts of our region. However, like Shigeru Ban, our school saw the need for conservation as the primary battlefront. And again this was a fight that no one could argue with. Not wasting resources, self-sufficiency, and resiliency are a part of Cajun and Creole culture.

Hector LaSala

PROFESSOR OF ARCHITECTURE AT UL LAFAYETTE AND ADVISER

Born and raised in El Salvador, Hector LaSala moved to the United States at age 16 to study engineering at Louisiana State University. After experiencing the culture of Acadiana, he left LSU, moved to Lafayette, and enrolled in the Architecture program at what was then called USL. He's been here ever since, teaching at UL Lafayette since 1976 and becoming a highly valued member of the community. LaSala is also an active participant in numerous environmental and non-profit endeavors.

"I was involved primarily as a supporter or adviser," says LaSala. "Geoff Gjertson and I went to the 2007 Solar Decathlon, and we noticed the majority of the houses were like BMW cars. They were really fine, but very expensive. So we started talking about doing it, but doing it right and building something that people can afford. We wouldn't solve any problems by just building something for the few."

HOPE:

"You've got to have hope, because it's the only way. Yes, it is sometimes difficult, but one cannot live without it."

Several of LaSala's ideas informed the regional yet modern emphasis of the home's design. "Modernism is misunderstood. It was born as reaction to all the things that were wrong with the established culture of Europe, so anything associated with innate culture was considered, in some ways, decadent by the modernists," says LaSala. "The initial architecture of modernism was void of any kind of cultural resonance. What we tried to do with the BeauSoleil Home is known as 'critical regionalism.' It attempts to correct that abstraction of modernism. The aim of the BeauSoleil Home was to build something that was contemporary but also evoked our culture – to somehow diminish the repugnancy that people feel about modernism."

In regards to the consumption trends in the modern world, LaSala has many ideas. "I think there is a correspondence between the depravation of living in suburbia and this kind of manic consumption in modern society," says LaSala. "People don't have a connection to cultural pleasures; therefore, they supplement it with nonstop television or consumption. It's an existential crisis. We've created a culture that doesn't know how to live. Buying and consuming is not the main purpose of living. Part of the mission of BeauSoleil Home is to create a community that inhabits an existence that is rich in its own right."

The timing was right, but the Solar Decathlon proposal was due in December 2007, just two months away. I was intimidated by the enormous engineering and technical side of the competition, but I knew we could find that local expertise. I was also intimidated by the fear that many of the universities entering the competition had participated in the Decathlon before and had started preparing for this proposal much earlier. Indeed the TEAM found out later that some schools already had a design at that point.

But there was no time for indecision or a lack of confidence. UL Lafayette was going to do this. And even though it was a highly competitive and selective proposal process, I intuitively knew that we would be chosen. It seemed providential. In 2005, the region had experienced two of the worst hurricanes ever: Hurricanes Katrina and Rita. Katrina was the costliest ($81 billion) and one of the most deadly (1,833 fatalities) hurricanes in history.[28] Rita affected our region of Southwest Louisiana more directly, making landfall a month after Katrina.

For the TEAM, the Decathlon was something we could do to help repair the devastation. As architects, it is ingrained in our DNA to help communities through design. As Samuel Mockbee, the MacArthur "Genius" Award-winning architect said, "Architecture is a social art."[29] Many architecture schools from around the country had gone to New Orleans to participate in charrettes and help build housing. UL Lafayette's Community Design Workshop, led by Professor Thomas Sammons, had done charrettes and master plans for the hurricane-destroyed towns of Cameron and Delcambre, Louisiana.[30] Although I wasn't quite sure how the Decathlon or the "Solar D," as we started calling it, would help, we had to continue trying to make a difference. [31]

So the fact that UL Lafayette was a mid-size university in the South, with no funding, no engineering team, and with only two months to write a proposal to the Department of Energy, did not deter us. We set our minds to it and followed through – even though it may have been somewhat naïve of us. However, for our soon-to-be-formed group, nothing could be more exciting. Even at that early stage, the opportunity of participating in an international competition with a Louisiana designed home seemed to motivate the individuals around me. Hope began to grow, too.

Assembling The TEAM

RECENT STUDIES HAVE SHOWN THAT ELITE ATHletes are not simply born with the right genes. Nor does the sentiment of "practice makes perfect" apply across the board. Optimal genetics in combination with hours of practice (10,000 hours is the tipping point often cited[32]) are required to be among the best.[ag]

Our entrance into the Decathlon, our journey, and our eventual success can also be attributed to "our stars" and our ways.[34] It felt preordained that we would participate due to the coincidence of all the factors cited above. But talent, planning, and hard work also played into this recipe for success, and serendipity added the spice.

First we had to submit a proposal and hope that we would be selected by the Department of Energy as one of 20 schools to participate (out of about 40-50 proposals).[35] I began the process by writing a position statement dated October 23, 2007:

Louisiana Solar House: A Marketable Application...The concept for the proposed 2009 Solar Decathlon Louisiana House is three-pronged: marketable, balanced, and contextual.[36]

Talk about the "cart before the horse!" I seem to have a gift for striking out on a path, even before I know where we are going. And based upon the past Decathlon homes, our need for affordable and hurricane-resistant housing, and Louisiana's rich culture of architecture, music, food, and dance, our direction was clear. "Marketable" meant two things: affordable and readily mass-produced. "Balanced" referred to the need for both active systems (photovoltaics, high-efficiency air-conditioning and dehumidifiers) and passive systems (natural ventilation and cooling). A balanced or hybrid approach was needed to reduce costs but more importantly to connect to our Louisiana traditions in terms of our way of life and historic architecture. The word "contextual" in the position statement refers to being appropriately designed for the climate and culture of South Louisiana.

Gretchen LaCombe Vanicor

STUDENT PROJECT MANAGER

Iota, Louisiana, native Gretchen LaCombe Vanicor was one of the first students to be associated with the BeauSoleil Home. Utilizing her degree in marketing/management, Vanicor's organizational skills and relentless motivation were highly valued strengths that came into play when multitasking a variety of situations, which included: delegating tasks, managing finances, reporting the TEAM's weekly progress to the proper agencies, and creating schedules for all those involved. Not surprisingly Vanicor is now Director of Sustainability at UL Lafayette. During the two years of the project, she was somehow able to maintain the morale of TEAM BeauSoleil even though she is not a psychologist.

"It's awesome to look back on the whole thing, but it was a hellacious amount of work," says Vanicor. "We worked all day, through the summer, and went to classes in between.

"Where I grew up, everybody kind of helped each other and passed on the trade. My father didn't think of himself in sustainable terms; he was just frugal. Unless it was really cold, we didn't put on the heater. Both of my parents were always connected to the landscape. I grew up in the country around a lot of farmers. My dad always had a big summer garden. My mom always did a lot of her own landscaping. In those ways, I was kind of primed for work on the BeauSoleil Home. But it was this project that brought me into sustainability. And it brought together a very diverse group that really unified over the project."

HOPE:
"Hope is longing for a positive outcome for the future and for your loved ones."

After getting University administrative approval to proceed with the proposal, I had to build a TEAM.[37] We decided early on to always write the word "TEAM" in all capitals. This emphasis recognizes the strength of the TEAM. Although this phrase is overused, the whole is greater than the sum of the parts. This discussion leads me to collaboration and service-learning (teaching through serving the community.) I fell into collaborative, design/build education. It came naturally because I love to build, and I enjoy mentoring young designers. This necessarily means motivating and leading a group of individuals to jointly complete a large task: a project. My leadership approach is not by dictating a design but by subtly guiding and creating an environment that allows for success. I prefer this definition of *facilitate* – "to smooth the way."[38] For example, I try to provide the resources and information needed to design and build, and then I get out of the way. The design process should be the student's own and not controlled by me.

During the first phase of building a TEAM, I asked for faculty support. Even though Professor Cazayoux had retired, he offered to help advise me and the students on the project. I asked the entire faculty, and everyone initially wanted to be a part of the process. For various reasons as time went on, only four other architecture and design faculty and one engineering faculty member remained active parts of the TEAM. As I was to discover, the nature of the Decathlon necessarily placed major responsibilities on a single faculty adviser as well as his or her student officers. In terms of writing the technical innovation and design narratives of the proposal, it fell primarily on Professor Corey Saft, Professor Eddie Cazayoux, Professor Brian Powell, and me. Professor Hector LaSala and Associate Professor Kari Smith developed the curriculum integration section, and Professor Jean Edwards served as editor.

Next, it was time to rally the students. Social media was still relatively new so I relied upon word of mouth to spread the message. Two students were attracted to the project immediately: Gretchen LaCombe Vanicor and Scott Chappuis. Interestingly, both of these students attended other universities for their undergraduate degrees in other disciplines. Vanicor went to McNeese State University in Lake Charles, Louisiana, for a marketing and management degree, and Chappuis went to the College of Charleston for a marine biology degree. Their Louisiana childhoods helped instill an appreciation of the environment. Addressing the issues of sustainability, architectural education, and community service with a single, large-scale vehicle like the Solar Decathlon, motivated them to become two of the leaders of the BeauSoleil project. Both possessed a pragmatic and rational approach that superbly served their interests and the TEAM's interests in the years to come.

Other students began to join the TEAM, with many of them becoming primary players. They included architecture students Denisse Castro Dufreche, Jeremy Credeur, Christopher Dufreche, Catherine Guidry, Greg Jefferson, and Chris Leger. Many others soon followed, including Timothy Dumatrait in architecture and Thomas Bosch in engineering.

In early November, the first iterations of the TEAM met on campus to conduct some initial planning. We had a great turnout: three or four students and five or six faculty. Excitement, or a kind of nervousness, was slowly brewing around the project. As varying factors came in to focus, the eventual members of the TEAM began to reveal themselves.

ABOVE
Architecture TEAM Officers

Although I would have liked the students to have had more involvement in the writing of the proposal, the deadline came too fast. On December 7, 2007, the final proposal was submitted to the Department of Energy. Corey Saft crafted part of the introductory statement that I still feel is succinctly powerful:

It would be difficult to find a more challenging or relevant condition in which to test building techniques and design proposals geared to meeting the world's upcoming challenges. Because of the recent catastrophes brought on by hurricanes Rita and Katrina our presence in South Louisiana has made us the team of experience. We have seen the FEMA trailer up close and in action, and have witnessed the ineffectiveness of current technology and response in the face of these disasters.[39]

UL Lafayette had to be chosen by the Department of Energy. It was that simple. Hurricane responsiveness and

Scott Chappuis

STUDENT PROJECT ARCHITECT

If you're going to build a home, you're going to need an architect. Scott Chappuis grew up in Lafayette's Saint Streets neighborhood and filled the position as one of the project's architects. After watching a documentary on the 2005 Solar Decathlon while working on an offshore boat, Chappuis decided to go back to school and study architecture. Strangely enough, a year or so later, he ended up working on UL Lafayette's entry into the Solar Decathlon, the BeauSoleil Home. His critical thinking and problem solving ability kept the TEAM focused throughout the project.

"I grew up in a great neighborhood with a lot of kids," says Chappuis. "I'm not sure how I got into sustainability, but I grew up hunting and part of what is so special about hunting is that you are going out and interacting with nature. Also, you don't kill more than you can use or eat. Later on, I worked on a sailboat, which is kind of a self-sustaining island in its own way. You're moving from one place to another using only wind power. We only had so much food and water, so you can't waste it. We had to take 'Navy showers,' where you run the water to get wet, soap up, and then run the water again to rinse off, and that's it. So I got in the habit of doing it, and I still do it now. From there, I began getting interested in environmental and sustainable ideas.

HOPE:
"Hope is to be excited and passionate about what is to come."

"Sustainability can be financially feasible. A lot of practices that were built into the BeauSoleil Home, like the overhangs, are older techniques. You think of sustainability as this new thing, but Professor Eddie Cazayoux's theories are all rooted in traditional typologies. Even if we didn't accomplish all of our goals, I think we laid good ground work for a step in the right direction."

LEFT
Katrina Satellite Image

MIDDLE
FEMA Trailer

RIGHT
Louisiana Coastal Marsh

resiliency, and the fight against rising sea-levels and coastal erosion, became important underlying themes for the BeauSoleil Home. We always saw the project as more than a single home but really part of a larger system or community that could help improve lives and the environment.

Following the submission, the TEAM had a well-deserved break over the holidays, knowing that we had put together the strongest and most compelling argument possible. In early January, the good news came. UL Lafayette was the first university notified by Jeff Soltesz of the National Renewable Energy Lab in Boulder, Colorado, that our proposal had been accepted and awarded $100,000.[40] I was thrilled and excited but also scared. What had we gotten ourselves into?

What's in a Name?

WHAT'S IN A NAME? A LOT. PEOPLE DO JUDGE A book by its title and cover. And although we did not need to sell our solar house for a profit, we needed to sell it for public acceptance of a more sustainable lifestyle and to help raise donations to compete in the Solar Decathlon. Moreover, by naming something you give it a conceptual grounding, a reason for being, and something to aspire to. If we could properly name our concept for the home, then our student design team would be better able to collaborate on a shared vision for the home. How should we begin? Aren't all the good names taken?

Over emails in November 2007, the faculty began to discuss the concept and name for the home. I began the debate by throwing out the name "the Rita Cottage" as a reaction to the Katrina Cottage in New Orleans. The Katrina Cottage was a mass-produced, historically styled, disaster-relief, modular home. The name "Rita Cottage" was just a place-holder for our home. But it was intended to be provocative and political. We wanted to continue to put Hurricane Rita in the public consciousness because Hurricane Katrina had so dominated the national press.

ABOVE
Hurricane Rita Damage

Two years after the hurricanes, we wanted the country to remember that the recovery was not over. And for me, "recovery" included the affordable housing shortage that had been exacerbated by the storms. Although things had moved faster in Southwest Louisiana than in New Orleans, the housing shortage was a continuing, long-term crisis, and we had not

ABOVE
Katrina Cottage Designed by Marianne Cusato

answered the question "what happens after the next hurricane?" We needed structures that could withstand the winds, be raised above flood waters, powered off-the-grid, and were more sustainable.[41]

Onezieme Mouton, one of our only faculty from Southwest Louisiana, felt particularly strong about references to Hurricane Rita, insisting that we not associate ourselves with the Katrina Cottage. Hector LaSala emailed Mouton in his typically thoughtful and diplomatic way:

Onezieme, you are correct about the sin-by-association to the banality that is the Katrina Cottage. On the other hand, we can show them how to do it right! I also want to make the point I made before: it is possible that the 'working title' may not (be) turned (into) our ... 'final name'. The process itself will tell. Also, one concern I have: as I visited the latest batch of solar decathlon houses in DC, I saw a template-like uniformity in them all (-) A modernity without the benefits and gains of critical regionalism. So, one name or another, the critical issue is to ground the project in our rich historical/cultural-climatic context and content.[42]

This theoretical and at times heated discussion went on for several days. Finally on November 4, Professor Michael McClure proposed the name "BeauSoleil" in an email:

The root of ecology is house. (The) amount of sustainability (active resilience) is in direct relationship to the amount of change the system can adapt to... maybe we should pretend like we are trying to name the band and start throwing out names to see what sticks... beau soliel (good sun?)...for music and culture, this is my newest favorite.[43]

Everyone seemed to know from the instant the name was proposed that it was right. However, we needed the approval of the Lafayette-based band BeauSoleil, especially if were planning to spell it as one word with a capital "S" as the band had done throughout its career. Both my cousin Todd Mouton and my colleague Hector LaSala knew BeauSoleil's leader and founder Michael Doucet. Each corresponded with him to get the required approval. Thankfully, not only was it OK, Doucet was honored to have his name associated with the project. As he stated in his email:

...this project is totally fitting with my own beliefs about creating creative housing that can be 'in tune with its

Michael Doucet

MUSICIAN, LEADER OF THE BAND BEAUSOLEIL

In addition to founding the two time Grammy award-winning musical group BeauSoleil, whose band name was adopted for the UL Lafayette BeauSoleil Home, Michael Doucet is a free-spirited, Cajun cultural ambassador at large. Considered by many to be the face of modern Cajun music, Doucet has appeared on dozens of albums, movies, and documentaries over the past several decades. The multi-instrumentalist's contributions to the region's culture are innumerable. In more ways than one, Doucet's lifestyle, conscientiousness, and attitude were a perfect match for the BeauSoleil Home and the regional scope of the project. To further emphasize the appropriate nature of this match, it was learned during the making of this book that the home that hosted Doucet's family reunions in the 1950s was named "Beausoleil."

"The beauty of the name Beausoleil is the idea of reestablishing or continuing an Acadiana society here in Louisiana," says Doucet. "So I had no problem being part of the BeauSoleil Home. I'm totally 100 percent behind it. Joseph 'Beausoleil' Broussard was kind of the guiding light who helped settle the Acadian people in Louisiana. He was a resistance fighter and leader. He did it for the people. So it's a very important name to our culture. It's historical and significant. And we should all know it."

HOPE:

"Hope shows you the mechanics of creation. People appreciate beauty. When they see it, they know it. There's something about beauty in any form that uplifts us. But you have to put heart in it. That's the thing about the BeauSoleil Home, it has so much heart."

No stranger to home improvement and local architecture, Doucet refurbished his own historical Acadian house years ago. "I restored an old Acadian house that was built in the 1820s – one of the three original houses of that vintage in Lafayette parish – on the original site," says Doucet. "I bought it for $100. I'm interested in Louisiana architecture as well as the culture, so when Geoff Gjertson told me about building a new house and using the name BeauSoleil, I was really into it."

BELOW
Joseph "Beausoleil" Broussard

BOTTOM
BeauSoleil avec Michael Doucet

environment and the culture of its inhabitants' and am honored that y'all considered BeauSoleil as a name of this project. I wish you and the UL School of Architecture all the best in this creative endeavor and I ask that I may see the model, if possible, and be kept informed of this unique development. BeauSoleil lives! [44]

"BeauSoleil" was perfect in so many ways. First, it meant "beautiful sun" (or just "sunshine" to the Cajuns and Creoles) in French. Second, it was the name of the Cajun band BeauSoleil, the Grammy-winning band from Louisiana. Since 1975, the band had served as cultural and musical ambassadors for Cajun culture, popularizing many of the best elements of Louisiana. Finally, the band, and by extension, our home were named after Joseph "Beausoleil" Broussard. The first French group from Acadie to settle this area in 1755 was led by Beausoleil, a charismatic and determined freedom-fighter. [45]

Meanwhile, I contacted Megan Barra, a local graphic designer, to begin work on the logo. The TEAM knew it was essential to properly "brand" the home from the beginning. I had seen Barra's work on album covers and other music-related graphics especially with the band BeauSoleil. There is a freshness, optimism, and lightness in Barra's album work that architectural graphics often do not have.[46] So in some ways, the desire to have a logo and name that appealed to a broader audience than just architects and designers drove the decision to use Barra. To pay for her work and the printing of the first brochures and signs, Holly and Smith Architects made the very first donation. I will always be indebted to them for their faith and trust in me.

On November 16, Megan presented the first iterations of the logo that eventually became the BeauSoleil Louisiana Solar Home logo. Barra's logo design perfectly encapsulated the simplicity of the concept for a home

BEAUSOLEIL
Louisiana Solar Home UL LAFAYETTE SoAD

that drew inspiration from the traditional raised Acadian house-form. The abstracted profile of the house, partially shaded by an oak tree and overlapping the sun, suggested the integration of architecture and nature - an architecture living with nature. Perfect.

Like the design to come, the name "BeauSoleil Louisiana Solar Home," was multi-faceted, had multiple-readings, and appealed to many different stakeholders. "BeauSoleil" relates to our French history and culture. "Louisiana" emphasizes that the home was contextual to our geographical location. The word "solar" is in some ways a hot-button word. Although solar energy is only a part of the solution to our energy problems it was not the most important design determinant in the BeauSoleil Home. However, solar energy is evocative of the early days of the environmental movement. So by including it in our name we not only connected to the Decathlon but also to the long history of sustainability.

Finally, the choice of "home" versus "house" intentionally references the adage that it is people and their belongings that make a house *a home*. They are more important than the bricks and mortar. "Home" is more personal, familiar, and intimate. It offers specificity.

For the first time in my career, and I'm sure for the first time in my students' careers, it was necessary to market and brand our ideas. Yes, architects have to sell their ideas to a client, but typically they do not have to make their designs appeal to a broader range of the public. We were attempting to market our ideas not because we were trying to make money (although we did need to raise funds); we were trying to perform public outreach/education and help promote a more sustainable way of life, and we hoped the home would be a prototype for many homes to come.

From the beginning, I posed a question to the students: how do you appeal to the broadest segment of the public while still being uncompromising in your vision for what the BeauSoleil Home should be? This was going to be a huge challenge. The proposed vision depicted an advanced, technological home that directly responded to our climate and culture. The mission was to balance avante garde modern architectural design with historical precedents and mainstream/popular culture. We now had a concept, name, and logo - we just needed a design.

Design

I BELIEVE DESIGN IS A COMBINATION OF THE canny (the everyday) and the uncanny (the unexpected). Our school teaches design this way. Another way to put it is a melding of the "poetic and the pragmatic."[47] All the information and research must be gathered and then combined with the intuitive process of play and exploration. Design is problem-solving. It is also a subjective spark of the imagination. Design can be premature, preconceived, and shortsighted if it is not grounded in research. We wanted the design for the BeauSoleil Louisiana Solar Home to emerge from a thorough understanding of all the issues and be animated by playful and creative expression.

The TEAM had its first strategy meeting on January 17, 2008, drawing most of the faculty and several students. The atmosphere was tense. It was time to delegate work. It was a situation I was to face in many faculty meetings over the course of the two year project. The faculty was supportive, but like all faculty in all disciplines, everyone has their own research and teaching agendas, and it is often difficult to all come together to work on one thing. But everyone knew that the competition required "all hands on deck."

Associate Professor Kari Smith and I started the senior design studio course with an emphasis on precedent studies and historical examples. We team-teach, which offers great advantages to our students by providing alternative view points. In my opinion, Smith has the second best definition of "sustainability" next to Shigeru Ban's definition. She says sustainability is "like a farm." What better example than a farm to encapsulate the complex interrelationship of the built and natural environment?

The students researched traditional vernacular examples, off-the-grid homes, homes in other tropical/coastal areas of the world, and prefabricated/modular examples. In addition we asked the students to study passive and active systems for saving and

LEFT
Cade Passive Solar House

BOTTOM
Precedent Diagrams

producing energy. Passive systems require no outside energy or equipment and were thus what our forefathers relied on. UL Lafayette has a long history of passive solar design with the Cade House, which was also funded by the Department of Energy in the 1980s.[48] The home was in need of repair and the senior design students inspected it, measured it, documented the passive and active systems, and made recommendations for its repair. Interestingly enough, we did not assign previous Solar Decathlon homes as precedents to research. Not that they weren't worthy but somehow they often represented a rule-driven design process that led to generic results. We later investigated the Texas A&M and Maryland houses for their successes in passive energy design and marketability, however.

Meanwhile, the development of the BeauSoleil Home website was launched by Reese Fuller, and the entire school had a two-week charrette on the Solar Decathlon to generate ideas for the home. The ideas ranged from an outlandish self-propelled spaceship-like home to versions of the traditional raised Acadian. We believe every idea has validity and should be considered on some level. We exhibited many of the ideas in our lobby. From this early point it was critical to have collaboration, ownership, and input from all stakeholders in the project. This meant not only the other faculty, but specifically input on the design from ALL the students in ALL primary design disciplines: architecture, industrial design, interior design,

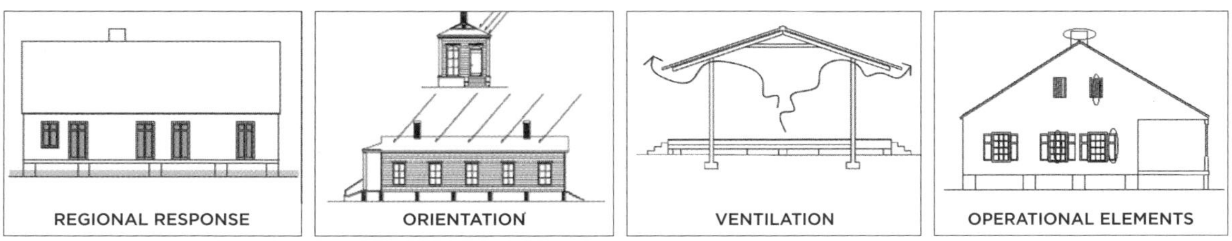

Kari Smith

ASSOCIATE PROFESSOR OF ARCHITECTURE

Kari Smith grew up in upstate New York on a dairy farm owned and operated by her family since the 1800s. She was the first of her family to attend a university. Smith is now the primary sustainability Professor of Architecture at UL Lafayette.

"There's something about putting big ideas forward in a competition studio where those ideas are not entirely fleshed out," says Smith. "You think big; you dream big. You're more visionary. I think that's what helped keep the momentum on the BeauSoleil Home going. I'm very interested in open source ware and the sharing of knowledge. I think that one of our goals was that this was a project that could serve the public. There's a real gap between what people can afford and what people want. I would like to see that gap shortened. The reality has to do with finances and a whole bunch of other things. But I think that working and being part of the community is inherently part of being sustainable. It's a lifestyle and an appreciation for the home that people can pass along to their children, and I think that's more important than the lifespan of the house. The house was a reflection of the team in that they were very family-centered and had a very strong connection to where they're from, and in those ways, it generated a very different result from the other houses in the competition."

HOPE:
"Hope is about the anticipation of something you really cherish. I think that was part of this project – the larger energy that people drew from. It wasn't just the end goal of the competition."

and engineering. And after the conceptual underpinnings were established by the students, we eventually wanted the input of the public and our design consultants to validate the design.

Throughout the design process, careful and honest interpretations informed our decisions regarding the design of the BeauSoleil Home. During the initial design phases, six biweekly public charrettes were held to test public perceptions and acceptance of the preliminary designs. Attendance was strong. It was clear that the public had opinions and an interest in the home, whether it was from those interested in solar homes, green building in general, or a uniquely Louisiana home that would win this international competition for our University. Everyone rallied behind BeauSoleil.

These charrettes provided us with useful feedback that described the unique needs and desires of our target homeowner. We gathered valuable insight from attendees whom we believe exhibited characteristics of both the median income range demographic for the commercialization model, and of the empty nesters (both single and married people whose kids had moved out of their house) demographics for the prototype model in the competition.[49] Similarly, informal personal interviews with others fitting these demographics provided additional information that helped us better understand the proposed BeauSoleil Home target segments.[50] These segments share an active, athletic lifestyle, appreciation for the arts and learning, and some college or undergraduate degrees, with middle incomes. According to an article in the *New York Times* by Stuart Elliot, the newest Baby Boomers are unlike traditional older consumers.[51] They are comfortable with new offerings and surroundings. BeauSoleil anyone?

SMALL HOUSE FOOTPRINT

ISSUE

Minimizing a home's literal and energy footprint is the first thing that should be done when planning a sustainable home. The average American family household has gone from 4 people in 1950 to 2 1/2 people in 2014, while the average house size has gone from 1,000 sf to 2,400 sf.

BEAUSOLEIL

800 square feet for 2 people, which can be added to as a family grows.

PROS

Reduced square footage allows for greater expenditures for higher performance A/C, lighting, solar PVs, solar thermal and envelope (see SIPs/Insulation sidebar). Transformative bedroom/studio with Murphy bed and desk integrated with storage/work area allows for easy and efficient storage of clothing and office supplies.

CONS

A home like BeauSoleil which is one-thrid the size of a typical home requires a change of lifestyle and reduction of belongings. Storage is the most commonly cited thing lacking in a small home.

As the design progressed, two things were first and foremost in my mind: the education of my students and providing them with the materials and resources necessary to be successful. To that end, with Eddie Cazayoux's help we invited Pliny Fisk III, Ed Mazria, and Dan Rockhill to visit. Fisk and Mazria had both been involved in the Decathlon and had written strong letters of support to the Department of Energy for us. They had been directly involved with past Decathlons as a competitor and as a judge, so they had specific applicable advice for the TEAM.

PREVIOUS PAGE
ARCH 402 Final Studio Review

ABOVE
Public Charrette

BELOW
Elemore Morgan Jr. Painting

Rockhill, an architecture professor from the University of Kansas, is one of the best known practitioners of design/build education. His Studio 804 designs and builds prefabricated homes and other sustainable buildings every year in Kansas.[52] The quality and craftsmanship of their projects is impeccable. I wanted Rockhill's take on our design and advice for coordinating construction efforts. He was shocked at the complexity of our design. This was scary coming from someone like him. Rockhill encouraged us to edit and simplify the design. We didn't! But it certainly made us more vigilant about focusing on the essentials. Overall, he was impressed with our TEAM and offered us much encouragement.

One of the most influential moments of the predesign/research phase was when Eddie Cazayoux and Elemore Morgan Jr. assembled Lee Ray LeBeouf, Rick Chargois, and Craig Morgan for a roundtable discussion with the student design team. All of these gentlemen and their families had lived off-the-grid (before it was a term) in the Atchafalaya basin and

the coastal marsh – not because they wanted to, but because they had to! For this reason they knew how to live with nature. From that point on Morgan became a confidante and inspiration for the BeauSoleil Home. Sadly, Morgan died in May of 2008, so he never saw the home completed. But fittingly one of his uniquely Louisiana paintings hung in the home in Washington, D.C., for the competition.

Chris Leger

STUDENT HEALTH AND SAFETY OFFICER

Chris Leger was born in Lafayette and raised on a gravel road, spending summers fishing in Toledo Bend, playing sports, and hunting in north Louisiana. As a child, he won so many school-sponsored art contests that he began to get disqualified by judges mistakenly assuming his parents had helped him draw his entries. Leger's love of the outdoors, strong leadership skills, and natural talent for art made him an ideal candidate for working on the BeauSoleil Home.

"I was one of the eight core team members who designed and constructed the home from start to finish," says Leger. "During construction of the home, I also oversaw general construction and safety issues. It was a unique challenge, overseeing hundreds of students that worked on the home in some capacity. In many instances these students had never worked with power tools, so keeping things running smoothly was a challenge. We were a regional school competing against some of the most prestigious schools in the United States and world. We were always up against the wall, pushing from start to finish. At some point, everyone wanted to bow out, but we kept it going.

"I spent many hours designing and working on the exterior of the home. I developed the exterior cypress cladding system as well as the window placement. I hand selected all of the cypress wood along with Donald Elder – a cypress milling expert and lumber yard owner in Opelousas. I also constructed the solar water heater above the Dogtrot space and countless other systems within the home.

HOPE:

"Hope is looking to the future where our thoughts and aspirations come to fruition and become life sustaining."

"For me it was the great sense of accomplishment in creating something real that would serve as a model for people to learn from and live by. We spend so many years in school theoretically creating architecture and honing our ideas of what that means to us. It was great to have gone through the process of creating something that would culminate into a built thesis project. It gave me a great deal of confidence moving forward."

ORIENTATION / LOCATION

ISSUE

After size, orientation and location are the two most important determinants of how sustainable a home is. Minimizing eastern and especially western exposure can reduce energy bills by up to 40%. Locating your home near deciduous trees for shading and a cooling micro-climate also reduces your cooling load. Finally, locating your home in an urban area reduces the drain on resources for infrastructure and transportation. (Roads and utilities cost $10 million/mile on average.)

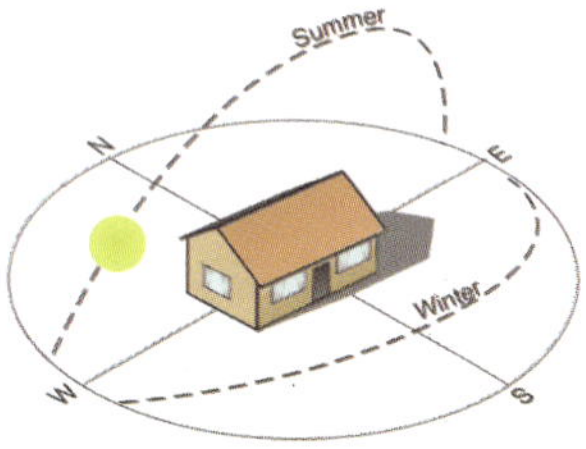

BEAUSOLEIL

The home is narrow in the north/south direction (only 14') which reduces heat gain on the west and increases passive ventilation. It is modular so it can be relocated as needed.

PROS

If designed into a new home these factors have no or little additional cost.

CONS

Urban in-fill property for single family homes is disappearing or unavailable in many cities. The BeauSoleil home cost $40,000 to transport 2,000 miles, an average of $20 per mile (typical base cost for moving a house is around $10,000).

Twelve students worked independently for six weeks to each generate a different design scheme. They produced plans, cross-sections, and three-dimensional models. By March 27, 2008, the students had each come up with the following typologies and designs for the home:

Gretchen LaCombe Vanicor and Denisse Castro Dufreche were inspired by the traditional Southern Dogtrot house form which has an open covered breezeway separating two parts of the home. There was a modern example in Zachary, Louisiana, designed by Stephen Atkinson. They particularly admired it for its simplicity, purity, and honest expression of materials.[54] This typology emphasizes the connection of the interior spaces to the exterior. Christopher Leger and Catherine Guidry also were inspired by the Dogtrot but had separate out-buildings to fulfill other functions of the home. This too was inspired by traditional homes but reinterpreted. Flexibility, modularity, and adaptation had become a conceptual underpinning. Jeremy Credeur and Chaz Kemp developed other multi-building schemes, this time with three separate units. This obviously allowed for

DESIGN QUESTIONS

In studio, the students were presented with questions to consider in addition to the 200 + page book of rules from the Department of Energy as they were designing the home.

- What constitutes a culturally resonant house form?
- What constitutes a "Louisiana house"?
- How does one design a "marketable" house without pandering to fashion?
- Understanding that a single home does not significantly address the housing shortage, how can the BeauSoleil Home begin to address the idea of community and/or multi-family living?
- If the BeauSoleil Home is to eventually be located in coastal Louisiana, how will it accommodate potential flooding/storm surge and hurricane-force winds?
- How will the BeauSoleil Home respond to the legacy of the FEMA trailer?
- What constitutes a design strategy of adaptation?
- What does it mean to be rooted in place while embracing the future?
- How can each component of the home be double-programmed or smart? [53]

LEFT
Zachary House by Stephen Atkinson

BELOW
Schematic Design Models

easier transportation of the components and allowed for extensive exterior spaces, but it also required more infrastructure. Timothy Dumatrait and Guy Brignac each explored two-volume schemes that were shifted but connected to create interesting exterior spaces. Christopher Dufreche and Scott Chappuis kept the form simple - a single volume. However, they both pushed the idea of clerestory windows and a more complex roof form to allow for passive ventilation. Passive systems drove their design thinking. Jean Paul Accomando developed an "L" shaped scheme, and Jaron Young had a linear scheme strongly influenced by the hurricanes - both in its deconstructivist form and focus on elevating inhabitants above flood waters.

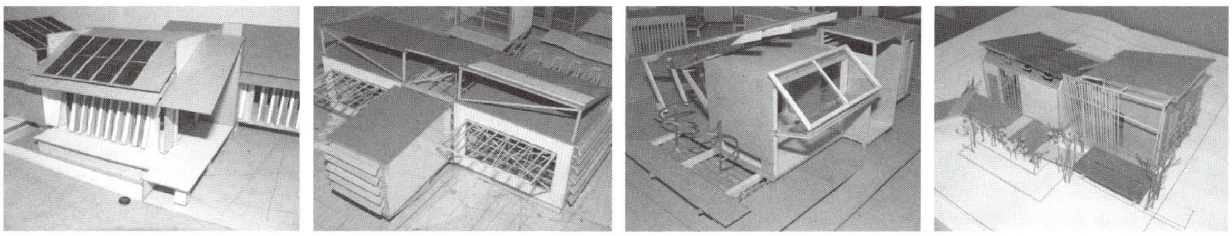

After the schematic design reviews were completed and each of the 12 students presented models and drawings from their concepts and typologies above, they were divided into two teams of six by the faculty. This division happened naturally because there were obvious similarities. One group developed the Dogtrot scheme and one group developed the S-shaped, two building scheme. After the second review, when these two schemes were evaluated by faculty and outside reviewers/consultants, the students voted independently to pursue the Dogtrot typology.

The elegant simplicity and functionality of the solution was best highlighted in the concept of the transitional porch

Tim Dumatrait

STUDENT DESIGNER / DISASSEMBLY CREW MEMBER

If you want to talk shop, Tim Dumatrait is the guy. Born in Lafayette and raised in the country outside of Breaux Bridge, Louisiana, Dumatrait was the first of his family to obtain a college degree. He spent many of his formative years learning to be resourceful and completing carpentry projects with his father, an avid hobbyist who worked a full-time job while raising a family and maintaining a wood shop, garden, and livestock. Articulate and blessed with a powerful intelligence, Dumatrait's focus on the design aspects of the BeauSoleil Home proved to be an invaluable resource as one of the project student architects who worked on the home.

"On some level, sustainability is a stigma," says Dumatrait. "We're an energy producing part of the country and it's very lucrative, but it's also very political. Everyone is trying to market products that are efficient, like electric cars, but at the end of the day, you have to plug it in. And that power is coming from a power plant, so that's part of the challenge.

"We're all trained to be designers and we all wanted to feel like our ideas were making it in – it's an ego thing. There were so many designs in the beginning; we probably had 12 to go through. Then it came down to two designs and we combined that into one scheme. Then we had to convince the people that weren't as enthusiastic about the final design that this was worth doing. The challenges toward the second half became the production of construction documents and producing a coordinated thing, making sure everyone's doing their job. But that's definitely what happens in the real world.

"Working on the BeauSoleil Home was an interesting journey into uncharted territory. I don't think any of us would have allowed anything to get into the project that would've been a critical failure. We all were after the same thing: a quality project that was well executed for the school."

HOPE:
"Everyone says that Americans don't make anything anymore, but it was our hope that said, 'We're going to design it; we're going to build it.' And we accomplished that."

(what the Dogtrot became known as because it could transition for different uses) - this is the only porch design that the Decathlon rules would allow. The rules required any area under a roof to be included in the maximum square footage of 800 square feet. Therefore none of the other teams had porches or even significant roof overhangs. Sliding doors could make the transitional space an interior space or an exterior space. It could enlarge the living room and kitchen if needed OR become an exterior porch. That was its beauty. The transitional porch became the heart of the house, its most identifiable feature, and everyone's favorite space.[55]

ABOVE
Design Development Model

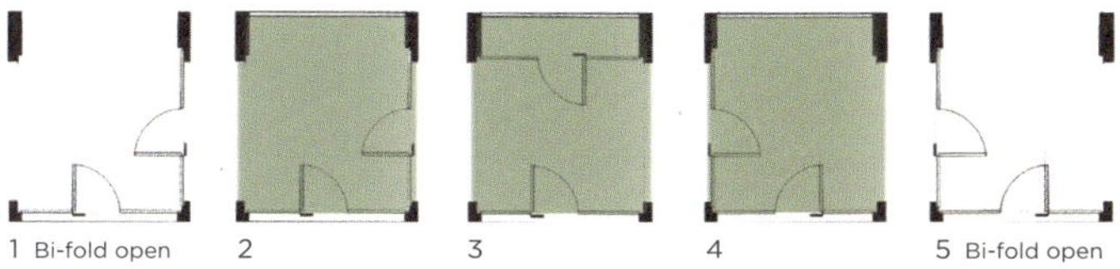

LEFT
Transitional Porch Door Configurations (In Addition to Breezeway Configuration)

It is important to stress that the design process was collaborative and decisions were made democratically by the students. They had ownership. It has been my experience that student-learning can suffer if the design is somehow, dictated by the professor and the students will not be motivated to pursue the successful completion and construction of the building. Individual egos and team spirit could combine to become an unstoppable force as the students are driven to see their designs realized.

BELOW
First Dogtrot Scheme Model

Following the end of the spring 2008 semester and the submission and acceptance of the schematic design drawings by the Department of Energy, the TEAM relocated from the fourth-year architecture studio to the interior design studio (upstairs at Fletcher Hall on the UL Lafayette campus.) This was the intensive research and design development phase of the project. Each of the eight architecture student officers and the two engineering students were paid as summer interns and charged with investigating a particular component, system, and material of the home. We had periodic group reviews and began collaborating with our engineering consultants and product manufacturers for input.

PASSIVE SOLAR HEATING

SHADING / DAYLIGHTING

ISSUE

48% of heatgain is from unshaded windows and 25% of your heating can be provided with winter sun. 70% of your lighting needs can be provided from natural lighting.

BEAUSOLEIL

2' deep overhanging awnings, operable shutters, and rolling screens properly shade southern windows. East and West windows are limited to only 6 sf of glass each.

PROS

The BeauSoleil home has the ideal East/West long-axis of the home. Window openings (53%) on South (42%) on North, and only (5%) on East/West.

CONS

Due to transport of the home there are no continuous 2' overhangs on southside. Only utilized awnings, which do not shade completely.

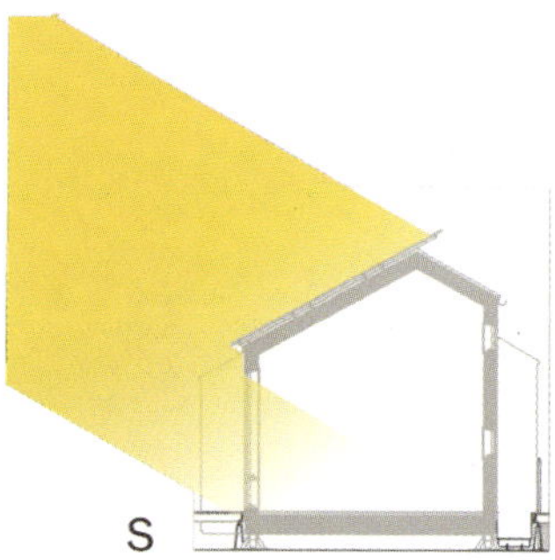

During the summer of 2008, the students got a crash course in traditional forms of passive ventilation and cooling. Professor Cazayoux took the TEAM on a day trip to visit historic Louisiana architecture sites and introduced them to the passive solar expert Pliny Fisk III. In addition, John Laudun from the English/Folklore Department spoke to the students about vernacular architecture. In this discussion, he spoke of the cultural importance of buildings and the individual components. In particular, gable roof forms connote domesticity, security, and childhood memories. As he said later in an interview, "Roofs have enormous social-capital."[56]

Months of design development followed. Materials had to be selected. Systems had to be tested and specified. Engineering studies were performed.[57] But the basic concept of a long, linear home with the central Dogtrot porch remained. Our final architecture narrative for the competition project manual best explains the origins and attributes of the design.

The formal composition of the BeauSoleil Louisiana Solar Home draws upon the vernacular Acadian Raised Cottage, Southern Shotgun, and Dogtrot housing types. In plan, the home is cruciform with circulation along the southern edge with the four primary spaces aligned. On the exterior, the tall, vertical proportions of the windows on the south, as well as the shutters, reflect these vernacular influences. The eastern facade, with its traditional symmetrical gable, suggests the iconic house form. The shifted ridge and shed-type roof on the west denotes the greater hierarchy of the kitchen within the home as well as promoting passive ventilation. The north facade, with its horizontal high windows, maintains the privacy of the occupants while allowing for passive ventilation. The expansion modules, which project from the main volume of the house, create additional space for an accessible bathroom/shower and the laundry closet. In addition, these forms are removable for additions on the home. The galvanized, corrugated metal siding of the expansion modules reflect vernacular housing and farm building types. On the interior, the high, vaulted ceiling height of 14' increases the perception of spatial size. Diagonal views through the spaces also increase this sense of spaciousness. A rich mixture of natural materials such as oak flooring and trim and cypress cabinets, as well as synthetic materials such as polycarbonate and anodized-aluminum, provide texture and warmth in the spaces. The Transitional Porch is the conceptual and literal heart of the home. Most activity revolves around and in this multi-functional space. The openness of this space (even when it is thermally enclosed) reflects the Louisiana lifestyle, which treasures entertaining and cooking.[58]

OPPOSITE PAGE
Visit to Pointe Coupee Parish, LA

BELOW
Computer Rendering

BOTTOM
Floor Plan

There are so many aspects of an integrated house design to consider – not just the more obvious design decisions like building form and exterior materials, but also decisions like the exterior landscape design, decks, railings, shutters and screens, and even flag-poles! Also on the interior, all the finish materials had to be selected. The furniture, artwork, and housewares needed to be picked-out (including the frying pan!). And of course daylighting or natural lighting was key in conserving energy, but artificial lighting can create spaces and change the mood of each room.[60] Interior Design Professor Brian Powell focused almost exclusively on lighting the home. As he wrote in the lighting narrative:

The lighting goal for the home is to create a relaxed environment that encourages socialization though the color and application of energy reducing technology. The lighting design for the BeauSoleil Louisiana Solar Home addresses interior lighting though three layers of light; ambient, accent, and task lighting... A rich and varied experience is created by the layers of light, by the use of three different lamp types (halogen, fluorescent, and L.E.D.), and by varying the lighting experience in each room.[61]

Powell worked with interior design students and Professor Charlotte Roberts to elevate the experience of the interior and connect to Louisiana.

Brian Powell

PROFESSOR OF INTERIOR DESIGN

Born in the small town of Marshall, Texas, Brian Powell was raised in the idyllic sanctuary of Friday night rodeos, roller rinks, and horse parades. To add further detail to the sleepy-town tranquility of his upbringing, Powell walked to school everyday, wearing nothing but overalls – no shoes or shirt – until the age of 10. His family eventually moved and settled in Shreveport, Louisiana, where his father worked as a designer at a landscaping firm. Now a Professor of Interior Design, Brian Powell was responsible for designing the lighting for the BeauSoleil Home.

"I feel lucky to have had this strong connection to nature in my upbringing," says Powell. "I think this is why the idea of preserving nature is so vital to me. If sustainability means preserving the joy of discovery I had in my youth, then I'm all about sustainability. My role on the BeauSoleil home included design of the lighting and interiors. Since energy efficiency was of utmost importance in winning the competition and making an example for sustainability, then efficient light sources were selected. L.E.D. and fluorescent sources are the only way to achieve efficient and sustainable lighting in today's and future homes. As far as the design of the interiors, it was a collaborative project with ideas and choices made as a team rather than an individual. Art from local artists was essential in expressing the regional nature of in our design solution so I got to work with several artists in the selection and placement of art."

Looking back on the project, Powell enjoyed the experience. "I like being a part of something that makes a positive effect on people's lives – including my own," he says. "Forming lasting connections with the team...especially the team that constructed the home on the Washington, D.C. mall was really rewarding."

HOPE:

Hope is the future. Projects like the BeauSoleil Home help us imagine a future that respects traditions and preserves the natural world – a sustainable future – one hopes.

The BeauSoleil Louisiana Solar Home graciously provided for the day-to-day rituals of life as expressed in our narrative for the competition project manual:

A day in the life of the BeauSoleil Home would go something like this: One awakens in a bed facing the west. Light can be modulated to enter the space with rolling blinds or exterior louvered shutters. Your bed can be folded into the wall, immediately enlarging and transforming the bedroom to a studio office. Cabinetry and a desk allow for easy and efficient storage of clothing and office supplies. The bathroom provides a buffer between the public living area and private bedroom area and sliding doors allow one to access the bathroom without venturing into the living area. When entering the bathroom, one is struck by the luminosity of the polycarbonate walls bathing the space in light. The warm and bright colors and tile convey a feeling of spaciousness and cleanliness. The plumbing fixtures and accessories are designed to accommodate everyone as they age through universal design strategies. The open shower is spacious and bright with translucent windows on the west and east. Both the natural light and mechanical ventilation limit the growth of mold which is a major problem in Louisiana. An efficient yet generous medicine cabinet stores one's toiletries and make-up close at hand. After bathing, one walks through the living room and outside through the Transitional Porch (unless the weather requires this space to function as an interior space.) By moving through the Transitional Porch, one is immediately put in close contact with the exterior environment and the changing temperature and light of the day. In addition, the Transitional Porch allows the kitchen to be separated from the main body of the house, thus prohibiting the heat of cooking to migrate. Additionally, the kitchen can be physically separated at night or at other times it is not needed, conserving energy. The kitchen is very large (160 SF) for an 800 square foot house and this is no accident. Cajuns and Creoles take great pride in cooking and entertaining in their kitchens. Our kitchen embraces this culture of entertaining and cooking. The vertical dimension of the kitchen is also the largest in the home which again glorifies and celebrates this important space.

BEAUSOLEIL'S FEATURES

Specific architectural features, elements and materials of the BeauSoleil Louisiana Solar Home include:

- Native plants and water features
- Cistern for water storage for irrigation
- Cypress rain-screen cladding
- Galvalume standing-seam roof
- Aluminum-clad wood, Low-E glass windows
- Roll-down insect screens which double as shading devices in the Transitional Porch
- Oak flooring
- Cypress cabinetry
- Reclaimed Ipe countertops (the scraps from the exterior wood deck)
- Translucent polycarbonate roof with integrated closed-loop solar water heater
- Reconfigurable, sliding glass doors/wall in Dogtrot
- Hurricane protection with operable steel shutters and a bifold hanger door
- BIPV's (solar panels) with parapets at roof edges
- Open floor plan with translucent bathroom module
- Transformative bedroom/studio with Murphy bed and integrated storage/work area
- Folding desk/work area in bedroom/studio
- Room for growth with Expansion Modules (shower and washer/dryer bumpouts)[59]

PASSIVE VENTILATION

ISSUE

Using natural air-flow can reduce the need for air-conditioning in Louisiana by 40-90% in the spring and fall. A/C uses the most energy in a home (50%).

BEAUSOLEIL

Using a traditional Dogtrot breezeway, air is pulled through the home by the venturi effect. In addition, low windows on the south (where the prevailing wind comes from) paired with high windows on the north also pulls air through the home through convection ("Suckulation" -Cazayoux).

PROS

The only cost associated with passive ventilation is an operable section and screens for windows which can double the cost of each window compared to fixed windows.

CONS

Although passive ventilation can remove pollutants it can also introduce dust, pollen, and humidity. Screens in windows reduce visibility. In addition, vigilance and monitoring to operate windows is required of the user.

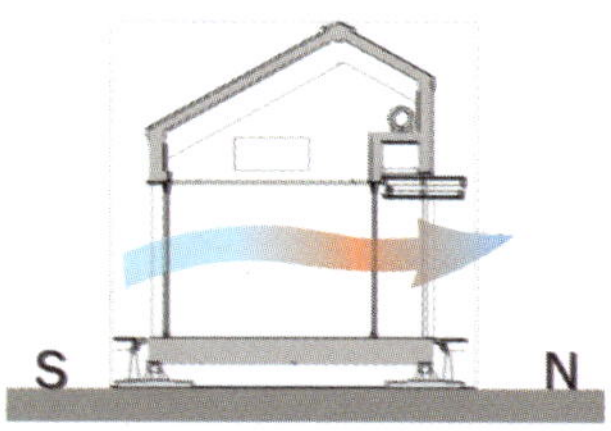

TRANSITIONAL PORCH

Also, a second set of high, north, clerestory windows allows for the expulsion of heat. Convenient placement of appliances and cabinets in the kitchen make this space highly functional. A vertical herb garden on the Kitchen porch allows one to get spices and herbs readily during cooking. After making breakfast, one can sit at the kitchen counter or dine al fresco on the Transitional Porch. The Transitional Porch also has roll-down insect screens to allow for it to be completely connected to the interior. If you have a guest staying with you, they can sleep in the Transitional Porch, which can be separated with the sliding glass doors.

When you go to work, your house is working for you, generating electricity and selling it back to the grid. When you get home at night the BeauSoleil Home is waiting to greet you with timed lighting features and vacancy sensors. Also, steel-grating, walk-off mats remove unwanted dirt and dust from your shoes before entering the home. Once inside, the three small ductless mini-split heating/air-conditioning units quickly and efficiently provide comfort exactly where it is needed. Additionally, a dehumidifier introduces fresh-air into the highly-insulated home to improve indoor air-quality. No-VOC paint also improves indoor-air quality. After dinner on the transitional porch you adjourn to the surrounding porches which effectively triple the size of this 800 SF home making if feel much larger than it is. Native plants and trees create a micro-climate and provide visual and fragrant enjoyment. As the sun sets, one enjoys the passive ventilation on the transitional porch and ponders the day. Like a sailboat, the BeauSoleil Home readily allows you to go about the rituals of life while at the same time enjoying and benefiting from the natural environment. [62]

AFTER DESIGNING THE HOME, we were not even halfway done. If you divide the two years of work on the BeauSoleil Home into its constituent parts, it would go something like this: 40% designing, 40% building, and 4% competing.[63] The remaining 16%, which was ongoing, was Getting the Word Out.

Getting the Word Out

THE MISSION OF PUBLIC INSTITUTIONS OF HIGHER education extends beyond the borders of their campuses. The University of Louisiana at Lafayette is dedicated to achieving excellence in education, research, AND public service. "The University promotes regional economic and cultural development, explores solutions to national and world issues, and advances its reputation among its peers."[64]

With the BeauSoleil Louisiana Solar Home we had the privilege of a national stage as well as the local limelight. So not only was it the mission of our project to conduct public service and outreach - to teach the public about sustainable design - but also an unprecedented opportunity to connect with dreams, desires, and hopes of our community; and to try to address international problems such as energy shortages.

Never in the history of UL Lafayette has a project garnered the attention that the BeauSoleil Home received. Our President, Dr. Savoie, even included mention of the project in two Commencement addresses. There is an incredible amount of good research and teaching going on at our institution so why did the BeauSoleil Home get so much recognition? It captured the imagination and propelled the hope of the community.[65]

We used the spotlight to teach, but we also leveraged it to our advantage to aid in fundraising. UL Lafayette, like most public institutions, was beginning to feel the effects of the recession in 2007-2009. The Louisiana state government began cutting higher education funding. When we received our acceptance letter from the Department of Energy in 2008, the University president at the time, Dr. Ray Authement, allowed us to compete with the understanding that University funds would be very limited. TEAM BeauSoleil would have to make its own rain.

Therefore, the challenge of raising the money for the home and the competition was always in the back of my mind. From research into previous Decathlons, we knew that about

$500,000 to $2 million had been spent on each home.[66] We were determined to build the home as affordably as possible without adding unnecessary frills. Still we had no real idea of the other associated costs to come, such as warehouse space, travel, or transportation for the home.

The name, logo, brochures, and website went a long way towards finding sponsors. The marketing was relentless, and many individuals were involved: Megan Barra, Andreé Gonsoulin, Dr. Denise John,[67] entrpreneur Robert Guercio, Dr. Geoff Stewart, the Russo Group, and on and on. Dr. John, our new marketing faculty member in the School of Architecture and Design, was in the ideal place at the right time. Her expertise in marketing was invaluable in the crafting of our communications reports and market viability narrative. We could not have done it without her. My challenge was balancing the emphasis on design with the need to market and sell the house and its ideas. Many will ask, couldn't the University administration help with this? This was a front that needed to be tapped.

John T. Landry, the director of development, helped raise money for the University. John T., as he likes to be called, had just gone through many of the statewide recovery effort meetings for hurricanes Katrina and Rita in 2007. As the TEAM sat down to meet with him in early 2008, he made the connection between what we were doing and the recovery efforts. Post-hurricane recovery efforts in Louisiana were inevitably tied to rebuilding with sustainable design. After all, sustainability also implies self-reliance, efficiency, and independence. And there was a lot of money being funneled into these efforts. If we didn't build better this time around we had missed a golden opportunity.

Immediately John T. referred the TEAM to Louisiana System Built Homes, which had just opened shop in St. Martinville, Louisiana. The company was to become one of the biggest supporters of the BeauSoleil Home and ended up donating the SIPS (structural insulated panels) shell and floor framing for the building.[68] In addition, they connected the TEAM with house-moving experts.

In April of 2008, the TEAM developed its first budget for the project, totaling more than $582,000. Of this, only $200,000 was allocated for the home. The rest was for transportation and all the other incidental items. The TEAM hired Andreé Gonsoulin to assist in fundraising by helping to craft the "asks" and making "follow-ups" as well as helping to plan events. Events and appearances began piling up - KRVS Radio interview, *La Louisiane*, American Institute of Architects South Louisiana Chapter Meeting and Charrette, Public Charrette, Earth Day, the Acadiana Open Channel, and *VOILA!* - when the design was revealed. An interesting and especially meaningful event was the family reunion for BeauSoleil Broussard's family in Maurice. The family was touched that we had adopted their forefather's name. We felt honored and obliged to best represent his heritage in the BeauSoleil Home.

ABOVE
Catherine Guidry During Interview in D.C.

OPPOSITE PAGE
Promotional Material

Catherine Guidry, the public relations officer for the TEAM, worked tirelessly to promote the home through interviews and presentations, TV and radio shows, sending e-newsletters and promotional mailings, and of course sending thank-you notes to our partners. This was a full-time job. And although she loved this aspect of the project, there were likely times she would have rather been working on the more typical aspects of architectural design and construction. However, Guidry is now a very successful professional photographer in Louisiana. I believe that the experience of the BeauSoleil Home helped prepare her for this career. As she expressed in an Department of Energy interview:

Catherine Guidry

STUDENT PUBLIC RELATIONS OFFICER

When it came to getting the word out about the BeauSoleil Home, Student PR Officer Catherine Guidry was on the front lines. Born and raised on the bayou in Morgan City, Louisiana, Guidry grew up in a resourceful, hard working Cajun household and spent her formative years around local lakes and immersing herself in the natural wonder of the landscape. Her infectious enthusiasm for the project served the team well when raising funds, conducting TV interviews, and creating awareness in the local and regional media. In addition, Guidry brought a highly effective level of professionalism to the project that brought out the best elements of the TEAM.

"I came from a pretty frugal family," says Guidry. "My parents always saved their money and in the process never wasted. We recycled cans, bottles, and plastic, and lived according to what was necessary rather than desired. Part of the reason I am passionate about sustainability is because it falls in line with the beliefs I developed growing up.

"We conducted hundreds of interviews, presentations, and meetings, and built a ton of awareness about the project. It was very rewarding being a part of the social media/public relations side for BeauSoleil, because it allowed us to not only raise the funds we needed but also inform others about sustainability. Those we presented to varied from 1st graders to the Chamber of Commerce and all proved to be equally as important in the eyes of the project. Although we may not have won the communications competition, we truly believe that we met the larger goal of educating at a local, state, and national level. The project brought so much awareness to our community; it wasn't just about the house, but about living sustainably.

"Although the Solar Decathlon created challenging restrictions through its rules and guidelines, it also provided a huge platform for us on The National Mall to share our message. It was an incredible experience that brought so much awareness to our University, our culture, and our state. And I hope that the concept of living sustainably continues to grow as a result of our participation."

HOPE:

"The BeauSoleil project gave us hope that living sustainably is possible. I learned so much over the two years about the practicality of incorporating sustainable practices into everyday life. And through the project I've developed hope that individually we can each play a small part in making the earth a healthier place to live."

My interest in architecture began when searching for a career that challenged the issues of society, resolving those issues with creative and innovative solutions. Architecture merges the practical with the impractical, the realistic with idealistic, and I enjoy the constant balance between the two. When approaching the time to decide on a graduate school, my decision was to stay here: to be able to continue enjoying the Cajun culture of Louisiana's food, music, and especially Cajun/Zydeco dancing, as well as to continue my work on the BeauSoleil project, which began in the spring of 2008. When placed into the position of Public Relations Officer, I was challenged with so many things that I had never done before (working with the media, presenting and speaking with an average of 3-5 community organizations, government entities, educational institutions, or businesses a week, and raising money for the project). As a result of the BeauSoleil project, I now have a strong desire to merge both sustainable architecture practices with both marketing and communications tactics.[69]

On June 25, we began work on a promotional film. Andreé Gonsoulin, our fundraising coordinator, had suggested that a film of this type could capture the richness and emotion of the project and portray it to potential donors. It could also be put on the BeauSoleil website and YouTube, which still seemed new in 2008.

At the close of the semester, several of us, including Gretchen LaCombe Vanicor, Scott Chappuis, and I visited Charles Richard and Conni Castille in the UL Lafayette Cinematic Arts Workshop's offices in the Whittington House, a big, old house across from Our Lady of Fatima Catholic School in Lafayette. Our Dean, Gordon Brooks, had suggested that Richard and company would be ideal for this project. He couldn't have been more correct. Richard and Castille seemed most interested in the emotions, back stories, and motivations of all those involved. The film crew interviewed members of the TEAM, asking them insightful questions about how and why they had volunteered to participate in a project of this scale and nature.

Several other team members were interviewed over the summer: Jeremy Credeur, Chris Leger, Catherine Guidry, and engineering student Jude Fusilier. At this point, the TEAM met videographer Allison Bohl DeHart and witnessed her shoot B-roll footage for the promotional film, which would serve as a backdrop for the story and flesh-out details and facts associated with it.

Many stories of the TEAM seemed to resonate with the film makers. In particular my personal story of dread with regards to the potentially dark future of our environment and my children who will inherit it, caught their attention. Another story that rang clear was Scott Chappuis's tale of working on a boat at sea and seeing a story on TV about the Decathlon and wanting to go back to school. The TEAM and the Cinematic Arts Workshop didn't know it at the time, but these stories would become the introductions to both sections of the film.

ABOVE
Promotional Video Filming

In the fall of 2008, the Cinematic Arts Workshop moved to the Louisiana Immersive Technologies Enterprises (LITE) Center in the University of Louisiana at Lafayette's Research Park. A few days prior to the filmed interviews, Richard sent the TEAM a script. We had no idea that this was part of the process of film-making. The script was composed of our transcribed interviews but Richard and Castille had crafted them into a beautiful and concise narrative. Every word was carefully chosen for its meaning and emotional impact. Although some corrections had to be made, for the most part they had captured the essence of the project.

However, it wasn't until we walked in their offices in the LITE center on August 18 that we realized how the message would look and sound. Each person took a turn sitting in front of the polycarbonate backdrop and camera, repeating our lines as Richard and Castille read them to us. It was an odd feeling to have to repeat your own words after they had been rephrased by someone else. It was especially difficult to repeat lines with the same intensity of emotion as they were initially delivered during the first interviews. For many of us, it was our first experience with acting and being in front of a camera. But in many ways it came natural because although we were essentially acting, we believed in what we were saying and felt passionate about it.

Bohl DeHart and Castille also filmed the TEAM at the warehouse in mid-September, while we were building an office in one corner of the vast workspace. Bohl DeHart's expertise as a cinematographer came into play as she shot the TEAM in action, operating saws and construction machinery under

Cinematic Arts Workshop:

Charles E. Richard, Conni Castille, & Allison Bohl DeHart

Like many other ambitious projects, fundraising is a necessary component of making the mission a reality. In the early design-stages of the BeauSoleil Home, Gjertson brought in the filmmaking team of Charles Richard, Conni Castille, and Allison Bohl DeHart from UL Lafayette's Cinematic Arts Workshop to assist in that area. The Cinematic Arts Workshop not only succeeded in kicking off the fundraising of the project in a highly significant manner, but also captured the collective passions, personalities, hopes, and motivations of the BeauSoleil TEAM members in a beautifully shot, nine-minute short film, which was dispersed through various media outlets.

"In the early days of the Cinematic Arts program, we had decided that we were going to focus on nonfiction and Southern Louisiana culture – play to our strengths – and the BeauSoleil Home had those strengths, so this was a good match for our interests," says Richard. "I knew this was going to work as a film when we started getting some of the personal stories from the TEAM members. With the BeauSoleil Home, you have an example of what universities can and should be doing, which is making things and learning through doing.

HOPE:
"The kind of hope that the BeauSoleil project offers the world is our stubborn South Louisiana insistence that we can adapt and flourish in even the most difficult environment without sacrificing the unique quality of life that makes this place home."

"Through the use of well planned shots and stabilized camera movements, we wanted the film to feel as well planned and well constructed as the house they were designing. Of course this film was going to be used to raise money, but there's nothing that said we couldn't make a piece of well made film, with good story telling and the best elements of documentary style and form. We wanted people to care. It's about sincerity. It wasn't simply about getting people to pull out their checkbooks. If you tell a good story and make a good work of art, the other objectives will fall in line.

"Culture is architecture. By appealing to the cultural roots of Louisiana, people really got behind the BeauSoleil project in the same way they get behind athletics. They were rooting for the project."

RIGHT
Promotional Video Filming

bright lights, capturing the energized activity in slow-motion as shop fans blew sawdust into the air. She asked for the warehouse lights to be turned-off so she could light the scene with spotlighting. It was a hot, sweaty, and surreal environment in the warehouse, one not that different in atmosphere from movies like *Apocalypse Now* where the filmmaker is shooting the battle in Vietnam, oblivious to the shells going off around him. What the film crew ultimately captured was the energy and teamwork of the project. And this was exemplified by the students raising a large structural, insulated wall-panel in the last scene.

The final filming occurred in the Fletcher Hall Auditorium on an evening in the late fall. The Cinematic Arts Workshop team had set up a dolly - a curved track for the camera to slide on. This was to be the introductory scene from the film. After several weeks of editing, the Cinematic Arts Workshop emerged with 9 minutes of carefully crafted video. The video is still on YouTube and has received more than 15,000 viewings.[70]

These are some of the most compelling lines from the original film script:

Guidry: *First, it had to be a uniquely Louisiana house. We're all born and bred here. So naturally we wanted a house that felt like home to us.*

Leger: *...So when a school from Louisiana was picked as a finalist, I think it kind of surprised a lot of people.*

Credeur: *A lot of times, Louisiana has a reputation for being kind of backwards. So BeauSoleil is a chance for us to change some minds and show that, in fact, Louisiana is a very progressive place. We can lead.*

This line "kind of backwards," delivered by Credeur was slightly controversial. In fact one of our sponsors asked that the TEAM take it out of future edits of the film because they felt it perpetuated a stereotype of Louisianians or Southerners in general. Unfortunately this is the perception of many people outside of Louisiana and it doesn't go away by pretending it doesn't exist. TEAM BeauSoleil was attempting to disprove it.

Guidry: *This project, being able to compete with these very prominent universities, gives us legitimacy, it validates our school, our way of life.*

Fusilier: *You spend maybe half your day in your house. The other half, you're out working to pay for it. With BeauSoleil, it's producing power all day while you're at your job. So the house is working for you.*

The role of the underdog served us well as a motivator and in raising public support. And this idea of making money from the sun has always been one of the solar movement's mainstays. Self-sufficiency was appealing to strong, independent Louisianians to say the least.

Gjertson: *Blending past and present, BeauSoleil summons a strong sense of place by finding uniquely regional solutions to regional problems.*

Vanicor: *To me, the most exciting features aren't the new technologies; it's the passive techniques, the ones that don't require any additional energy. A lot of them are things that our ancestors understood very well.*

The idea of rediscovering ways of building which our forefathers had used seemed to resonate with many people. There is an honesty, simplicity, and obvious rationale to this approach.

Chappuis: *Simple things that we've forgotten, like knowing where the winds come from, where the sun rises and sets.*

Gjertson: *Following hurricanes Katrina and Rita, there has been a growing awareness in Louisiana of the need for self-sufficiency, for sustainable housing designs, and for energy independence.*

The theme of resiliency and independence tempered by

sympathy for past hardships endured, appealed to a national audience. The storms had made us tough.

Gjertson: *More than other Americans, perhaps, the people of South Louisiana have become especially aware of the fragile relationship between people and their environment.*

Fusilier: *In modern society, more and more, you feel a disconnect from your environment. You're in your climate controlled home, you're in your climate controlled vehicle. You're in your climate controlled business. So you live in a bubble.*

Breaking the bubble of modern life and reconnecting people to nature and to other people is a message well-received by many in today's interiorized and virtual environments.

Fusilier: *...All these things that create a connection to the environment that our ancestors enjoyed, and we've lost.*

Gjertson: *Designing a home is much more than just creating a space to shelter a family from the elements. Good architecture shapes the relationship between people and their surroundings—both the natural environment, and the social environment.*

Credeur: *We put a lot of emphasis on the kitchen area because as a group we believe the kitchen is the most important room in a house in Louisiana.*

This last line was juxtaposed with a scene from Credeur's family cooking and eating gumbo. The kitchen is a symbol of comfort and stability not just in the South, but elsewhere.

Guidry: *The Solar Decathlon is a chance for the world to look at Louisiana in a new light...*

Vanicor: *...BeauSoleil is our chance to shine.*[71]

Everyone was completely taken with the effectiveness and emotional content of the BeauSoleil promotional film. I'd be willing to argue that a Wall Street advertising agency couldn't have done a better job with a $2 million Super bowl commercial budget. Why? This was REAL. Real people and real emotions. This is how the TEAM truly felt, and by extension, this is how many people in the community felt.

The film was first screened and approved by the TEAM in October and then printed on DVDs in mid-November with a

beautiful cover design by Megan Barra. The TEAM showed the film to the UL Lafayette President Dr. Joseph Savoie and the University Council (Administrators) on November 3. Shortly after the release, a big premiere was held at the Alumni Center called *Reunion des Amis* (Gathering of Friends). The *Reunion des Amis* was a high-power event with congressmen and many donors from the region in attendance. The film had a tremendous effect and many of those in attendance were moved to tears by the scenes. In fact, even though I have probably seen it over 100 times it still has an emotional effect on me.

Even with this compelling video running on our website and on YouTube, countless hours were spent promoting the project. Out of our $827,915 total budget ($261,489 cash, $275,526 in-kind, and $290,900 grants), we estimate that we spent about 15% (or $82,000) doing public relations and marketing.[72] The fundraising was truly grassroots, and this can be evidenced by the fact that a very large majority of the donors were in the under $1,000 range.

But as of September 2008, the TEAM had only received $45,390 in cash donations to the UL Lafayette Foundation for the BeauSoleil Home. Some of these early Partners were: Holly and Smith Architects, the Gulf Coast Recovery Fund, Louisiana Manufactured Housing, LUBA Insurance, the Louisiana Architectural Foundation, American Institute of Architects Louisiana Chapter, the American Community Renewable Energy

DONATIONS

$4-999	140 donors
$1,000-4,999	40 donors
$5,000-9,999	24 donors
$10,000-24,999	8 donors
$25,000-99,999	11 donors
$100,000 or more	2 donors [73]

ABOVE

Stills from Promotional Video

Fund, and our UL Lafayette alumni association in Washington, D.C. Most of these donations came from personal calls or "asks" by me and Catherine Guidry.

Besides design and engineering classes devoted to the BeauSoleil Home project, marketing classes were coordinated with our fundraising and branding efforts in September 2008. We began scheduling many presentations, but the TEAM was also constantly getting requests to speak. Overall, the TEAM had no fewer than 100 meetings and presentations each of the two years of the project (2008 and 2009.) Marketing materials included brochures, flyers, postcards, hand stamps, bumper stickers, billboards, a website, a blog, an online newsletter, t-shirts, CDs (with a BeauSoleil song), DVDs of the film, stickers, buttons, pens, and 10,000 grocery bags with the logo that were distributed to visitors of the home in Washington. The TEAM had incentives or "perks" for "partnerships" (this word was used instead of donations or sponsorships to establish an intimacy with the TEAM) such as naming rights and partnership levels (Live Oak, Magnolia, etc.)[74]

ABOVE

Leger at Booth at Festivals Acadiens et Créoles

RIGHT

Vanicor & Guidry Accepting Donation from Acadiana Mortgage Lenders Association

OPPOSTITE PAGE

Accepting Check from UL Student Government Association

Even though we already knew how much work fundraising events required, we had three more events in the spring of 2009. We were gluttons for punishment. There were more efficient ways to raise money, but these events were the best at raising awareness of the project and sustainability. We held the AIA Sporting Clay Tournament on March 21, *Bike for BeauSoleil*

on April 4, and the AGC Golf Tournament on May 1. We also chose to hold these events because outside organizations agreed to host them on our behalf, with the exception of *Bike for BeauSoleil*, but we did have the help of the Acadiana Biking Association. Jeremy Credeur's wife, Michelle, did an incredible job organizing this event. It was a lot of work but all together the events generated about $20,000.

As a part of the D.C. experience we decided to try to bring the band BeauSoleil. This was an obvious but complicated plan to enact. It was a drawn-out process of negotiations and contracts with their agent/promoter. We finally struck a deal and the Lafayette Convention and Visitors Commission paid for BeauSoleil to make the trip.

As we moved closer to the competition date we scheduled our hotel and met with the University administration regarding funding for student travel. Ken Ardoin, the Vice-President for Advancement, suggested an Adopt-a-Student campaign of $1,000 per student to cover many of these expenses. Brilliant!

On June 7, 2009, we received a huge, unexpected donation, $50,000 from the UL Lafayette Student Government Association. We were expecting them to present a check for $15,000. When they said it was for $50,000, I was blown away. My jaw literally dropped, my legs became weak, and I couldn't stop crying tears of joy. I was truly shocked and moved.

The Russo Group developed a new message with talking points based upon the branding we had already done. Stacy Grow with Russo did an amazing job for TEAM BeauSoleil. The Russo Group added an emotional, almost spiritual plea with the mantra "Believe." At the time, I actually felt it was a bit dramatic, but a majority of the TEAM liked it. And to their credit, the Russo Group had identified, even at this early stage, the idea of "hope" in the project. For although the word "believe" refers to an individual's singular assertion of a truth or opinion, and "hope" seems to have a broader connotation, both words speak of budding potential and optimism.

Here are excerpts from the promotional message dated April 9, 2009:

There comes a time in everyone's life when they choose to believe. They dare to imagine the impossible - challenging the expected while turning dreams into reality. For a select group of students from the University of Louisiana at Lafayette, believing has not only changed the way they see the world, but quite possibly, the world we live in as well.

Beginning in the fall of 2007, students from UL Lafayette began working on conceptual designs and applications for the BeauSoleil Louisiana Solar Home. BeauSoleil, which means "Beautiful Sun" in French, or "Sunshine" in Cajun French, proved to be an ideal choice for their team and project as they worked to design a culturally relevant, technological hybrid that advances the traditional homebuilding in our region.

With this mission in mind, the UL Lafayette design team worked to capture the essence of Louisiana's rich cultural heritage in their design. The transitional porch and kitchen respond to the region's love of entertaining and cooking. Native plants and local materials, such as cypress, were incorporated throughout the home and landscaping. For the competition, the home will be completed with Louisiana artwork and performances by a local Cajun band.

As the BeauSoleil Home takes its place on the global stage, it will take with it the history and tradition of an entire culture. TEAM BeauSoleil believes in our University, our culture, our state, and our future. The world will believe too when they experience Louisiana in a whole new light.

There comes a time in everyone's life when they choose to believe. Today, we invite you to join us on this journey - today, we invite you to believe.[75]

WITH THIS NEW MARKETING APPROACH WE EMBARKED on an extensive public relations and community-outreach campaign. Just in March and April of 2009, we presented our message and film to: the Rotary Club, LITE Center Design Week, the 705 Young Professionals, a Brownie Troop, the Freetown - Port Rico Coterie, the Acadiana Realtor's Association, UL Lafayette Enrollment Services, and a local TV morning show, *Passé Partout*. The funny thing was, we were so passionate about the project and to share what we were doing, we often forgot to solicit donations. We really were trying to educate the public not just about our home but about sustainable design. And I guess this is really what it was about, generating hope and optimism.

We had over 2,500 Facebook fans, over 200 news articles, and a 60% brand awareness among the public. Over the course of the two week competition in D.C., we had over 26,000 viewings of the beausoleilhome.org website. And the BeauSoleil Louisiana Solar Home video offerings have had more than 30,000 plays - more than any other individual home in the Decathlon.[76] In regards to public awareness, we certainly got the word out.

Building BeauSoleil

FROM THE STUDENT OFFICERS' THESIS DOCUMENT:

The planning is over and it is time to find out if all the preparation will pay off. ...The knowledge base of the student labor ranged from experienced carpenters to those who had never held a hammer. ...These students would learn through the process of constructing this home, how to build, how to work with subcontractors, how to solve problems, all of which will make them better architects. Through the heat of the summer when the warehouse felt like an oven, the work continued on and every day brought a new challenge, and with each challenge came a new lesson...every aspect of the home made the TEAM better.[77]

The students remember it well, as do I and the other faculty who worked on the BeauSoleil Louisiana Solar Home in our warehouse. The 12,000 square foot United Way warehouse was a lot of things to the TEAM. It was a huge responsibility. Although the rent was discounted it was not inexpensive - about $40,000 for the year. But it gave us independence. It was sort of our "skunk works" (where the U.S. government secretly developed the stealth fighter in the 1970s) off campus where our maverick group was pursuing innovation.[78] Most importantly it gave us all

a place to keep our resources secure and close at hand - and weather would not slow us down.

We needed a big building to construct the home. United Way of Acadiana was looking for non-profit organizations like us. United Way totally supported the University and TEAM BeauSoleil's mission. They even had a large roll-up door installed to accommodate the BeauSoleil Home.

Within the huge shell of the building we constructed an interior space to do design work, carry out desk work, and meet with people. This space was built from donated plywood, framing, and windows. Many of these materials came from one of our neighbors, the Habitat for Humanity ReStore. Another neighbor, the Lafayette Second Harvest food bank, lent their forklift to us when needed. The office space ceiling was enclosed with a plastic tarp and two small AC units helped cool the interior.

We had an office area with about six computer workstations and a conference room with a big table from the old city newspaper building. Fabian Patin, a local architect who was closing his office, donated all the other furniture we needed. Just outside the office space we built cubby-hole shelves for tool belts and hardhats. The big warehouse was divided in two by the placement of the home. Tools were located on one side and material storage was on the other. A webcam kept tabs on us through the entire one-year construction process.[79]

On September 3, the TEAM moved into the warehouse. Luckily the Louisiana Department of Natural Resources donated most of the first year's rent for the warehouse. On September 10, the governor's wife, Supriya Jindal, visited the BeauSoleil Warehouse and our official ribbon-cutting was held on October 1, 2008.

Immediately we worked to complete the construction drawings for the BeauSoleil Home. At the same time, the computer drawings and files required to cut the Structural Insulated Panels were being prepared by Jeremy Credeur and Scott Chappuis at Louisiana System Built Homes in St. Martinville, Louisiana.

OPPOSTITE PAGE
Warehouse Ribbon Cutting

ABOVE
Warehouse Office

BOTTOM
Construction Webcam

Jeremy Credeur

STUDENT CONSTRUCTION MANAGER

Jeremy Credeur was born in Lafayette and grew up in the country outside of Carencro, Louisiana. He spent his early years fixing things on his family's property, including assisting in the construction of an addition to his father's house. After four years in the Navy, working on a ballistic missile submarine and spending months at a time living under the sea, Credeur studied architecture and graduated from UL Lafayette. Credeur was one of the core members of TEAM BeauSoleil, adding a healthy competitive element and drive to the group.

"I grew up around a very mechanical and self-reliant family," says Credeur. "The BeauSoleil project was definitely a good experience. It was experimental, but it was real world experience. While building the house, we learned how to adapt a lot of materials to do things that they weren't necessarily designed to do. At times there were some arguments, but 99% of the time, everyone got along. That says a lot about the core group of people that were involved in the project through the whole thing. I think there were 10 of us total that pushed it on through.

"I liked the materiality of the house – the way it felt more like something that everyday people would live in versus something that was like the Glass Box concept. I think experimental types of construction, like this project, benefit the construction industry. That's definitely a plus. I don't know if the BeauSoleil Home is a model for what construction could be in the future. I don't know if that is the answer, but at the same time it was a good experiment. Until you try things and until you go through the process of building something, you don't know how well it's going to pan out."

HOPE:
"Hope is being able to envision something and then strive to achieve whatever it is you are trying to do. And it inspires people to create things and think outside of the norm."

Unfortunately, just prior to cutting the insulated panels in February, we found out that they needed to be properly structurally-tested in order for the Department of Energy to approve them for use on the National Mall. As one can imagine, with thousands of visitors in the homes, safety was of the utmost concern to the organizers. Val Domingue, the manufacturer's representative, provided sufficient test data, and paired with the certification of our structural engineers, Ray DesOrmeaux and Randall Hebert, we were able to overcome this hurdle. DesOrmeaux taught civil engineering to our architecture students at UL Lafayette and Hebert occasionally partnered with him on projects. We were grateful that Hebert came with us to Washington, D.C., as our on-site engineer.

LEFT
Deck Framing

There were also internal conflicts amongst the TEAM. Any big project will have its ups and downs. I didn't know it at the time, but there were several occasions when students threatened to quit because of the stress. Our TEAM officers worked their magic to keep us intact. This is the ultimate testament to the dedication of the TEAM.

The project consumed us. We could never do enough. There were innumerable tasks to plan and accomplish as deadlines approached. In addition, the need for funds constantly hung over our heads as the intensity of our schedule loomed. We all worked from sun-up to sun-down. As Brian Powell

3/23/2009

4/01/2009

4/08/2009

5/01/2009

SIPS / INSULATION

ISSUE

Insulation and weatherstripping offer the greatest return on investment (R.O.I.). Poorly insulated homes can lose/gain 50% of heat.

BEAUSOLEIL

6 1/2" SIPs (Structural Insulated Panels) were used for the walls and 10 1/2" SIPs were used for the roof. The SIPs are made with 1/2" OSB on each side of E.P.S. (expanded polystyrene).

PROS

SIPs are 200% stronger and have a 33% greater R-value than fiberglass insulation in traditional stud walls. SIPs are erected 55% faster than traditional framing. Electrical outlets and switches can be precut in panels or easily cut-routed after erection.

CONS

SIPs cost 20% more than traditional framing. E.P.S. is flammable and it is difficult to locate plumbing in SIP walls. The total costs for SIPs on the BeauSoleil home is $15,900. E.P.S. is very slow to biodegrade.

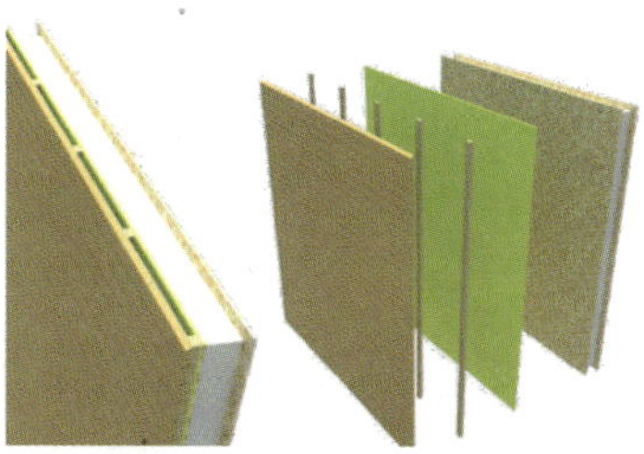

said, "Geoff could never leave!"[80] For me, the excitement, and enormity of the challenge was an effective motivator. Eddie Cazayoux conveyed the ultimate compliment when he said, "I never saw you stressed out."[81]

We did make time for enrichment, however. The students and I visited the Shangri La Arboretum in Orange, Texas, designed by Lake Flato Architects. This was one of the few U.S. Green Building Council's certified buildings in our area.[82] And we took a trip to New Orleans in November to visit Byron Mouton at Tulane to see the URBANbuild houses his students had designed and built to help neighborhoods. This was inspiring to see for both their social content and their actual tectonics of construction.[83]

In January 2009, eight students, Dan Burkett, and I attended the Solar Decathlon Pre-Event Workshop in Washington, D.C. This was a chance for all the teams to meet face-to-face, ask direct questions of the organizers (DoE and NREL), and of course visit the National Mall. This was an exhilarating experience to finally confront and meet the other teams who we had only known by name or through their voices on our monthly teleconferences. I think we realized that we were all pretty much alike with the exception of the German team, which seemed older, wiser, and more serious than everyone else. During a break, we walked our future building site on the hallowed National Mall and measured with strings the size of the home and approximate ground elevations. We were convinced we would be arrested as terrorists or spies!

When we returned to Lafayette, Scott Chappuis and I continued weekly engineering meetings in Dr. Bob Henry's office with his engineering students. Dr. Henry was the only active

engineering faculty member involved in the BeauSoleil Home, and he dedicated much of his teaching and research time to the project.[84] He was tireless and worked hand-in-hand with his students - even getting on the roof to install PVs. And, Dr. Henry and his wife, Billie, even drove their RV to Washington, D.C., for the competition!

Besides building we were constantly searching for money. We only had a portion of what we needed. We had raised $90,000 plus the $100,000 from the Department of Energy at that point. We would eventually need two times that much cash. Mike Hollier with the Lafayette Consolidated Government, a long-time partner with the school, suggested that we ask the Lafayette Public Trust Financing Authority for a donation. I had never heard of this entity. Gretchen LaCombe Vanicor and I presented twice to them. At the second presentation, on February 11, 2009, the public trust voted to give the TEAM $125,000. They donated $100,000 in cash and $25,000 for advertising with the Russo Group. As a TEAM, we felt truly blessed and relieved. We still had a ways to go but we were now more than halfway there.

Another huge milestone occurred on February 17, 2009, when the shell of the BeauSoleil Home (framed floor and rough insulated wall panels only) was transported to our warehouse and rolled into position over the temporary piers. It's hard to explain the satisfaction and excitement this generated for the TEAM. We had been working on the project for a year already and the house was finally taking shape. I remember spending the afternoon with the primary student officers just sitting in the spaces that would become the rooms of our home. There really is nothing like being able to finally occupy spaces you have previously envisioned, drawn, and then created. This is what we had been waiting for. There was great satisfaction and hope. We took a group photo that is still one of my favorites.

OPPOSTITE PAGE
Laying-out Home on Mall at Pre-Event

ABOVE
Moving Shell of Home

5/11/2009

5/13/2009

5/19/2009

6/05/2009

Dr. Robert R. Henry

PROFESSOR OF ELECTRICAL ENGINEERING

Born and raised in Crowley, Louisiana, Robert Henry spent countless days on his father's acreage where he learned about the multitude of tasks required of a farm, including raising cattle, tending the land, and gardening. Henry received his undergraduate and master's degree in Electrical Engineering at UL Lafayette (then known as USL). Later, he worked for NASA on the Apollo missions, doing communication systems design. Henry eventually obtained his Ph. D in electrical engineering from New Mexico State University and has been teaching at UL Lafayette since the mid-70s.

"I was faculty adviser for the engineering team," says Henry. "I guided the students and worked with them on the electrical engineering aspects of the home – primarily the PV panels and electrical system, in addition to the system that measures the power being produced and consumed by the house, which would show us if we were using more energy than we were producing.

HOPE:
"Hope implies the future. And I know from the lessons we learned in this project, if we apply them to habitats, we can create hope."

"The most rewarding part of the project was working with the students and seeing them design and create a solar system that was competitive. It worked well; the house produced more energy than it consumed. This was our first time to the Solar Decathlon. I expected us to do pretty well. Our design was good – both the architecture and engineering.

"The actual competition was 10 days, but you were given three days to set up and one to take it down. Fourteen days start to finish, but we were there at least a month, arriving before to bring it up and get it ready to go. One of the issues we had was the inverters that converted the solar DC energy to AC stopped performing during the competition. It turned out it wasn't our fault. All the houses on the mall were pumping energy back into the grid, but we were at the end of the line, so it shut off our inverters. We also had a problem with some receptacles that were wired in a row and tripping, but the students resolved the issue. It was miswired and potentially could have kept us from competing, but the students got it all fixed. They really came through."

Following this euphoria, we realized two days later that we built the floor framing of the house 4" too narrow. Always the level-headed officer, Scott Chappuis tried to calm the TEAM, diffuse the situation, and bring everyone up to speed.

(Chappuis email to TEAM):

Hey everybody, I am writing to talk about the fact that the base of the house was built at 13' 1.25" wide instead of 13' 5.25" wide...I think considering how much we have to change if we continue with what we've got we'll actually lose more time than if we stop and fix it now. All this said, I don't think we should get down on ourselves. We've put in an incredible amount of work and this is everyone's first time doing this kind of thing. I also don't think we should point fingers; we just need to support each other and move on. Mistakes will be made and we just have to learn from them and hope as we get smarter we'll catch most of them ahead of time.[85]

ABOVE

TEAM BeauSoleil in Shell of Home

The miscalculation was not anyone's fault. It is a common occurrence when rushing under pressure to build something. We all made a mental note to be more careful in the future. As the old adage says, "measure twice and cut once." Our solution to this problem was to move the wall. On Ash Wednesday after Mardi Gras, we moved the south wall over 4" by placing solid 2x12 blocking below. This allowed the wall to be moved out 4" without having to reframe the floor. If anything, this solidified our resolve to avoid letting the occasional mistake bring down the spirits of the TEAM. And it made us stronger.

On March 4, we held the *Building BeauSoleil* Commemoration. Lafayette City-Parish President Joey Durel posted the building permit and our priest Father Chester Arceneaux, blessed

6/11/2009

6/25/2009

7/06/2009

7/20/2009

RAINWATER HARVESTING

ISSUE

An average of 36,000 gallons of rainwater are wasted on a typical homeowner's property each year. Cost of water in Lafayette, LA, can range from $1.59 to $3.18 per 1,000 gallons in 2014.

BEAUSOLEIL

The $2000 system consists of 100 LF of 6" half round gutters, 4" downspouts, and a 700 gallon cistern. A valve is available for water or can be connected to irrigation system. The system collects 0.62 gallons of water per square foot of roof area, per inch of rainfall, however there is usually some loss due to evaporation. The system for the BeauSoleil home can collect about 26,100 gallons of rainwater per year. (0.62 x 0.85 x 800 x 62 = 26,100 gallons per year)

PROS

Inexpensive, saves $62 per year on water, keeps water from splashing against house. Attached to a drip irrigation system to water plants.

CONS

Not filtered, not used for greywater because local ordinances prohibit use of rainwater for potable (drinking) or even flushing toilets.

the home. Interestingly enough, no one ever questioned the appropriateness of having only a Catholic priest involved versus religious leaders from multiple denominations. I guess it is because about one-third of the population in Louisiana is Catholic.[86] Father Chester wrote a beautiful prayer just for the blessing that was published in *La Louisiane* magazine.[87]

By April, it was getting hectic, and we were two to three weeks behind the construction schedule. If you've done any construction, you know that there are inevitable delays in ordering materials and getting subcontractors to show up and do their work. And then every task takes twice as long as you think it will. So in many ways this was expected but still disconcerting considering all that was at stake. I was getting burned-out, and I took a much needed short vacation. Of course, BeauSoleil was never out of my mind, and I continued to do work via email, communicating with TEAM members and monitoring the progress of the house.

Dr. Bob Henry developed a computer-generated energy-model and found that our energy consumption was too high vs. our production, in a precursor of future problems. We addressed this shortfall by making some reductions in energy usage by deleting light fixtures. Problem solved. Next. There was always a next. If another minor problem does not soon reveal itself in short order, an individual in charge of a project this size can become even more unnerved at the ominous quiet of negative potentialities lurking in the shadows of some future disastrous scenario. Thankfully, we were able to deal with each problem in a somewhat calm and logical fashion, befitting a university and its attendant gallery of experts.

The school year ended in May, but we continued to work as if nothing had changed. The intensity of our schedule brought out the best in the TEAM. I worked five days a week in the warehouse, 7 a.m. - 5 p.m. In addition, we had the primary seven or eight TEAM officers and an additional three or four students working all summer. All five faculty worked an average of 100 hours per week total.

The TEAM also began discussions about placing the home next to Fletcher Hall after the competition. Other possible locations being considered were an Eco-Village in Opelousas, the future I-49 Sustainability Park, the Vermilionville Living History Museum, and the UL Lafayette Horse Farm. The Freetown-Port Rico Coterie (neighborhood association) even presented a proposal to the TEAM and University to permanently locate the home along the Atakapa-Ishak Trail in Freetown. After exploring all options, the TEAM voted to keep the home on campus near Fletcher after the competition.

OPPOSTITE PAGE
Father Chester Blessing Home

TOP RIGHT
Vanicor Carrying Cypress Siding

BOTTOM RIGHT
Credeur & Chappuis Installing Roof

In my haste to thank some members of the TEAM for the extra time they were putting in to complete the communication plan and construction documents that were due in mid-May, I failed to recognize others for their work. Keeping everyone happy in a group this size, can be its own full-time job. As I often had to do during this project, I apologized. I really wanted everyone to feel appreciated and just get along. They truly were an outstanding TEAM. Here is my email:

Thank you for everything you've given to this project. I am not exaggerating when I say we could not have done this without each of you. Please forgive my heavy handedness at times. I really, really appreciate you and I know everyone else does as well.[88]

Obviously there were many, many tense moments over those two years. As the faculty adviser, I was constantly telling the students that this was THEIR PROJECT. I really believed that, and I still do. However, I know at times I occasionally overstepped that boundary when something had to be done differently and

8/13/2009

8/21/2009

8/24/2009

8/24/2009

Rev. Chester Arceneaux

TEAM PRIEST

Southern Louisiana's roots are not only steeped in the structures of our man-made surroundings, but in the deep spiritual faith that has ushered the community through generations of challenges, hardships, and triumphs. Father Chester Arceneaux was asked to bless the BeauSoleil Home and accompany the TEAM to Washington, D.C., for the Solar Decathlon. A native of Lafayette, Father Chester has a Bachelor of Arts in Philosophy and a Master of Arts in Divinity. He was ordained as a priest in the Diocese of Lafayette in 1992 and has continued his ministry in Louisiana since that time. His calming presence and bighearted personality brought an element of emotional stability to the TEAM that helped them focus on the bigger picture.

"Sometimes we try to put God in a glass box," says Father Chester. "Although the Catholic Church is my faith, I was there for everybody. The experience of the BeauSoleil Home showed the universality of God. It was a spiritual pilgrimage. It was amazing to see so many new ideas. And I was so impressed with the TEAM. I think we continually evolve. We're not the same people we were 100 years ago. But I think we continually evolve into how creation can bless us and how we can bless each other.

HOPE:
"Hope is the ability to know what we possess and to strive for it."

"There are challenges in all things; it's really a test of spirit. With the resources God has given us, we're expected to be good stewards of the earth. BeauSoleil brought out a consciousness of our stewardship for our world. When I was asked to bless the home, I thought it was a great privilege and honor. For me, the nature of the project was based on the proper use of God's gifts and utilizing them to their fullest potential."

we were approaching a deadline; moreover, I was ultimately going to be held responsible for any failures of the project. As a society, we collectively celebrate victories, but in the event of a loss or some disastrous failure, someone's head will unfortunately be placed on the proverbial chopping block. In this case, it was primarily mine, so for the greater good of the TEAM, the University, and our community, I did my best to avoid that conclusion.

TOP RIGHT
Dogtrot Solar Water Heater Roof

BOTTOM RIGHT
Leger Working in Dogtrot

Here is another example of a difficulty one may face when taking on a project like this. Near the end of construction, Project Manager Gretchen LaCombe Vanicor and Construction Manager Jeremy Credeur called me into the office as we were getting close to finishing the installation of the plumbing systems. The plumber was a very nice young man from St. Landry Parish named Robert Bergeron. He had complained to them that he was being sent to the job before there was work to do. As is my methodology, I had been putting pressure on Bergeron and his boss to complete the job. The job's got to get done. Let's do it. Vanicor and Credeur were concerned about Bergeron's perception of being pestered and maybe the additional monetary costs associated with his coming out several additional times.

But in this case, we were building a complex house with multiple energy systems and a lot of other logistical issues that needed tending to. I have a theory. And my theory is that "pestering" is what you have to do to get subcontractors to show-up when you need them. That's how you get the job done. I am less worried about offending them and more concerned with getting the job properly done within the confines of the budget, schedule, and to the best of our collective abilities (probably my theory about relationships throughout a lot of the project). Sometimes feathers get ruffled.[89]

It's not that I don't respect contractors; most of them do a stellar job under very stressful conditions. But many times I have

8/24/2009

8/24/2009

8/24/2009

9/25/2009

TOP
Gjertson Teaching in Home

ABOVE
Home Under Construction

OPPOSITE PAGE TOP
Leger Carrying Cypress Siding

OPPOSITE PAGE BOTTOM
Home Under Construction

witnessed them promise something, and then not show up for days. Where'd they go? Who knows? Some subcontractors have a deeply ingrained defense mechanism, buried far back in the winding aqueducts of their DNA, which seems to make them say what they think you want to hear, and not necessarily what they believe. As it turns out, in this case, I may have pushed the plumber too hard, because we blew the budget for plumbing labor, and we still did not have time to fully test the system.

Meanwhile construction continued with the installation of the wood siding on the outside of the home. The new-growth cypress used on the BeauSoleil Home is a unique story in and of itself. During the summer of 2008, when the design team was doing research and design development in the interior design studio at Fletcher, Chris Leger was assigned the exterior skin and windows of the building. The design decision had already been made by the TEAM that cypress would be used. In many ways this decision was obvious. Our vernacular buildings always made use of cypress due to its availability and rot/insect-resistance. Traditionally cypress was used in thin 3/8" to 3/4" thick by 6"-8" widths. These boards were then lapped one upon the other from the bottom up. This siding was installed directly on the framing without sheathing (or plywood - because it wasn't readily available until the 1920s) and without a water or air barrier/membrane.[90] The entire cypress skin was allowed to "breathe" because it was unpainted and unsealed (no caulking) and it was installed somewhat loosely (with gaps) over open studs or half-timber frames. This allowed the wood to dry properly and quickly after getting wet, extending its life.

In addition, the cypress traditionally used on buildings was from old-growth trees. The large bald cypresses pulled from the basin and swamps were enormous - 5-10 feet in diameter and over 100 years old. These old-growth trees had very tight growth rings and were thus much denser than new-growth cypress. Unfortunately, the old-growth cypresses are gone. If you want old-growth material it is typically antique salvaged material which is very expensive because it is coveted for furniture and decorative interior elements (beams, flooring, etc.) So, when Leger began searching for cypress, we realized that for

SOLAR THERMAL WATER HEATING

ISSUE

Using the sun to pre-heat water for homes can reduce electricity costs. Water heating and air-conditioning are the biggest consumers of energy in our homes. Solar Thermal Systems cost $4,000 to $8,000

BEAUSOLEIL

The closed-loop solar water heating system is integrated into a prefabricated structural roof system with skylights. The flat plate collector utilizes aluminum fins (like airplane wings), painted black (to absorb more heat), and placed between two layers of polycarbonate). It costs $6,176.58 and produces 140 degree water on a sunny day. According to Energysaver.gov, a solar water heater like ours will generate between $13-20 per month savings while reducing your water-heating bill by 50-80%.

PROS

The system also allows daylight into the space.

CONS

The use of solar thermal requires a backup electric instantaneous heater, unfourtunately it cannot produce 15 gallons of 110 degree water in ten minutes when daylight is not available. The system also requires maintenance twice per year.

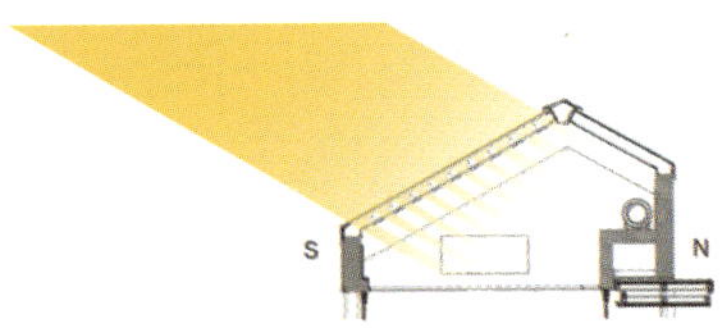

affordability and marketability, new-growth cypress was the way to go. But how would we extend the life of this less-dense and thus less-rot-resistant wood?

European architects and builders developed an exterior building skin system in the 1940s and 50s which came to be known as a rain-screen.[91] The idea is that instead of trying to keep water out the cavity between the exterior skin and the back-up wall, a rain-screen is designed to limit the amount of water that enters the cavity, but most importantly, to allow the cavity to easily drain and dry-out. This is done through carefully placed joints, gaps, or weeps in the system. Also, a larger air-space or cavity between the exterior skin or rain-screen and the water/air-barrier below is used. The rain-screen system seems to be a perfect modern adaptation of the traditional lap-siding which was allowed to breathe in the old homes of Louisiana. In addition to the rain-screen system, a penetrating sealer and a top-coat sealer were used to help preserve the new-growth cypress of the BeauSoleil Home.

TOP
LaCour House, Pointe Coupee Parish, LA

ABOVE
Cypress Siding

FOLLOWING PAGE LEFT
Chappuis & Vanicor Installing Siding

FOLLOWING PAGE RIGHT
Pushing Home Out of Warehouse

As Leger continued his research he found several potential sources of cypress north of Lafayette in Opelousas. One supplier, an older gentleman named James Donald Elder, was particularly enthralled with the concept of the BeauSoleil Home and offered to help. We had no idea at the time that he would assemble a supply-chain team of logging companies, lumber mills, and a finish mill which could produce our siding.[92] Eventually the unique siding shape was trademarked "BeauSoleil."

The all important moment had come; the siding was to be installed. For me, this was the moment of truth. This was the last thing installed on the outside of the house and certainly the most visible. This is what you would *see*. From hearing stories of the rigor of Dan Rockhill and his university design/build class,

Christopher F. Dufreche

TEAM CONTACT / STUDENT PRODUCTION ARCHITECT

Born and raised in the country town of Pumpkin Center, Louisiana, Chris Dufreche is one of those small town guys with a ton of ambition and the brains to match. A childhood fascination with science and a job working at an architecture firm as a teenager brought him into the world of sustainability and design, which made him a perfect candidate for TEAM BeauSoleil. Dufreche's focus, organizational skills, and energy were prized assets of the project. His primary responsibilities, among many others, included coordinating construction documents and participating in the design of the home's passive solar water heater.

"Even as a child, I always had a strong tie to science," says Defreche. "I think technology is really pushing architecture forward as far as sustainability goes. It's making architecture more responsible not just in regards to the environment, but economically.

"I'm an extrovert. I feed off of people. And I truly believe that any project is better through collaboration with others. That is a value I had before, but I didn't realize it as much until after the project. And it wasn't just the home. It was that sense of camaraderie that we did this. If I had to sum everything up in one word, I would say it was collaborative. There were so many different elements. Yes, there was a core team of about eight to ten of us that saw the project from its infancy all the way to the Solar Decathlon. But I cannot count how many people touched this project from the very beginning and from all different majors. Everybody had the right attitude. We weren't working against each other. We were working with each other to create this awesome thing. And we had so much support from the community. They had hope and faith in us that we would represent them with a wonderful, beautiful, and amazing project."

HOPE:

"Hope is really faith. You wake up everyday, hoping that you can not only make yourself happy, but others."

Studio 804, I knew it was an option to take off the siding and start over if it wasn't straight.[93] So if anything, I was consciously trying to be even pickier than usual because sometimes in the past I had accepted "Just OK." But this was the Decathlon and the BeauSoleil Home, and by all accounts, we wanted it to be the best it could be.

And that's exactly what happened. Several TEAM members had installed about half of the cypress rain-screen on one corner of the house when I returned from a meeting. The officers and I noticed immediately that it was not plumb or level. There was no yelling or screaming. But it was all taken off immediately, and Scott Chappuis and Gretchen LaCombe Vanicor took over the siding installation from then on out. Their workmanship and craft was amazing - perfectly level, with perfectly centered and countersunk stainless steel screws.

From July to August 2009, we had an exhibit at the Artists and Architects Gallery in Downtown Lafayette titled *E'volution BeauSoleil*. The purpose of the exhibit was to chronicle the design process of the home and help illustrate the final product, including the art which would be displayed in the home. This event provided a pleasant respite from the severity of the routine in which we were immersing ourselves on a daily basis.

ON THE FIRST DAY OF SCHOOL IN THE FALL 2009 SEMESTER at 9 a.m., the home rolled out of the warehouse and into the sun. This was the biggest milestone yet. The home was basically complete, but now we needed to test it in the light of the sun in order to check our solar PV panels and, more important, our

SOLAR ELECTRIC PVs

ISSUE

A typical southfacing roof on a home can generate 800 kWh per year which powers 20% of an average 2 bedroom home's needs, saving $440 per year.

BEAUSOLEIL

7.8 kW Sanyo System with (26) 215 W panels, (13) 205 W bifacial panels, and (2) Xantrex 240v inverters, costing $35,000, placed at optimal angle of 30 degrees (Approximately 6:12 pitch) facing due south. This system is net zero for the 800 sf home. Excess energy is returned to grid during day, and the home draws from grid at night. PVs are mounted to a galvanized steel channel (uni-strutt) that is clipped to the standing seam of the roof.

PROS

Will last at least 25 years at full efficiency with only once-per-year cleaning.

CONS

Expensive. Conservation of energy with high performance insulation and high efficiency appliances/light fixtures will offer a greater return on investment. Micro-inverters are more efficient than regular inverters because they maximize the power from each PV panel vs. averaging the efficiency among all the panels.

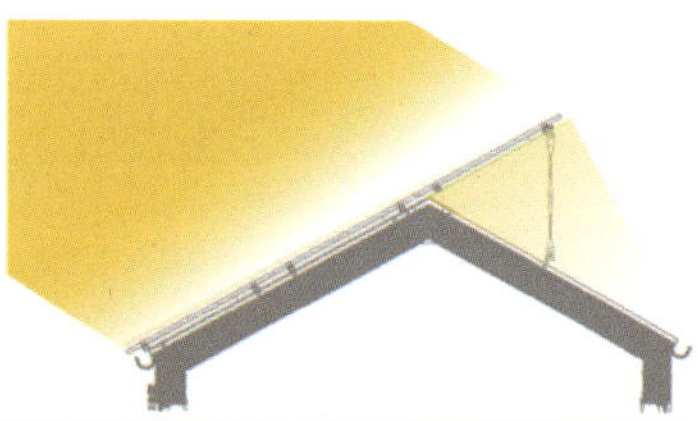

solar water heating system. Minimal tests were completed and the systems checked-out ok. However, we failed to simulate each and every one of the Decathlon contests. This would come back to haunt us.

During one of our visits to the St. Martinville modular home manufacturer we met Ken Thibodeaux, also known as Keno (pronounced "Kino"). Keno was as true a Cajun as I have met: a genuine salt-of-the-earth man - sincere, funny, industrious, and hard-working. Keno had been moving homes and trailers for decades when the manufacturer hired him to move their homes. He and his brother worked together with various truck drivers and hired hands to move and set-up modular homes throughout the South. Keno is one those unique individuals, who for whatever reason - whether religious or preordained naivety - doesn't let the details worry him. He just has faith that things will work out, and he intuitively knows that worrying isn't going to make a lick of difference.

Even though Keno had no experience with solar or alternative energy, he instinctively understood the importance of our endeavor. And he could articulate it in a no-nonsense way: "You're trappin' the sun in! It all starts with that, saving energy. The way we're going, we're going to have to do something for energy."[94] He got it.

When the shell of BeauSoleil was complete, it was inevitable that Keno would move it to our space at the United Way warehouse. Without surprise, it was a relatively easy job. Collectively impressed with Keno's magical ability at moving seemingly immovable objects, we broached the subject of

MINI SPLIT HEAT PUMP

ISSUE

Air-conditioning and heating are usually the biggest energy consumers in a home. Mini splits are more efficient because traditional split systems require ductwork which accounts for a 30% energy loss and provide one zone (one thermostat) in a home.

BEAUSOLEIL

The home has two 1.5 ton Mitsubishi mini-splits and one 2 ton mini-split which share one condenser. This allows individual customization of heating and cooling in each of the three zones (kitchen, living room, and bedroom). The cost of the system including labor is $11,089. Complementing the HVAC system with a dehumidifier ensures comfortable humidity levels and allows for the introduction of fresh air into the home. In addition, during the mild months in the fall and spring, the dehumidifier and passive ventilation is the only climate control needed.

PROS

A single small condenser for multiple zones and variable air-speed and cycling (start-up) utilize 50% less energy than comparable split systems.

CONS

The system cost 2 times more than typical split-systems. Typical split-system size is 400 SF of house per ton; the system for BeauSoleil is twice the amount of tonnage for an 800 Sf home.

L.E.D. LIGHTING

ISSUE

L.E.D. lamps (bulbs) last up to 30 times longer than incandescent bulbs. A 50,000 hour lamp used 8 hours per day will last 17 years. Add to that, less energy usage, less heat, no mercury, no UV light, resistance to shock and heat, and a better focused light source.

BEAUSOLEIL

The home uses 34 L.E.D. fixtures, 17 compact flourescents, and 17 halogens. The light fixtures for both exterior and interior cost $14,729, averging to $18.41 per square foot (800 SF). The lighting goal for the home is to create a relaxed environment that encourages socialization though intimacy and application of energy reducing technology.

PROS

The low energy-use, space-saving size, shock resistance, and low-heat aspects of L.E.D. were most important in BeauSoleil.

CONS

L.E.D. lamps cost 3 to 4 times more than incandescent bulbs and their bright white light can wash-out the color in people's faces (bathrooms) or in food (kitchen). In addition, they require transformers which have the tendency to trip GFIC circuit breakers.

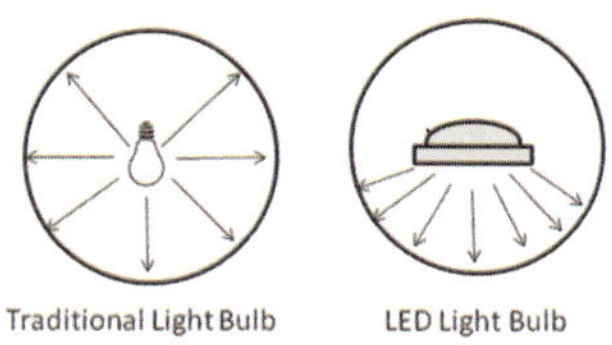

Keno possibly assisting us with the BIG MOVE to Washington, D.C., and back. Without hesitation Keno said he would do it.

Keno came to help us roll the home out of the warehouse on little casters. Talk about scary! He and his brother lowered the home onto these small wheels. They then slid the home perpendicular to its length, and began squeezing slowly through the roll-up door of our workspace. But it was just outside the door that the difficulty arose. The pavement abruptly dropped away and the home had to tilt and potentially bend until we were back on level payment! The extreme weight (approximately 40,000 pounds or 20 tons!) broke one of the casters, and the home became nearly impossible to move. Under Keno's direction, we somehow managed to nudge the house out with a Bobcat while pulling it with a truck. Keno and his brother were true heroes on this day.

Deadlines were approaching; it was crunch-time. After we pulled the home out of the warehouse, we geared up for a test disassembly on August 31 which for all intents and purposes was a dry-run for the competition assembly. The idea was to take the home apart and put it back together. Lafayette Steel Erectors sent a crane over to remove the roof sections. After

John "Keno" Thibodeaux

TRANSPORT SUPERVISOR

The French-speaking John "Keno" Thibodeaux comes from both Boudreaux and Thibodeaux stock, but he ain't no joke. Born and raised in Breaux Bridge, Louisiana, and no stranger to building things, he built his first house after moving out of his parent's home and lived in it for 33 years. Thibodeaux was instrumental in transporting the entire BeauSoleil Home 1,195 miles to the Solar Decathlon in Washington, D.C. Blessed with an intuitive intelligence, Thibodeaux is one of those naturally brilliant, salt of the earth guys who can level a house with a garden hose and figure out a way to do any number of things if given the task. His patience, when problem solving, was one of the greatest assets to the TEAM.

"I always did like a challenge," says Thibodeaux. "And I've always been interested in new things, like solar power – it draws my attention. I worked with a lot of people over the years and you don't often get a chance to do something like the BeauSoleil Home. I've worked in housing for 32 years and I never went through a project like this. It was completely different. And I'll never forget it.

"When traveling that far, with that much house – a lot of things could go wrong. But we didn't have hardly any problems. Everything went good. My biggest problem was safety and trying to figure out how we were going to do the roof – as in how to put it on, take it off, and put it on trucks and then deliver it to Washington. That was a challenge. It was all done with kids who'd probably never worked in the field before. But I got to say; they did a great job. The BeauSoleil Home did good things for Lafayette and the area. Most importantly, it showed them what kind of people live and work here. And that it's not just a party."

HOPE:
"Hope is the opportunity to get to do something again...and to be a part of it."

unbolting what we thought were all the plates, the crane tried to lift the biggest section. It strained several times, but could not remove the roof. After double and triple checking the assembly, we realized several plates and bolts were still in place. We removed them, and the roof came aloft. Overall, it worked perfectly. The three sections came off without a hitch and without collapsing (folding in half!) as I had feared in my nightmares. Putting the roof sections back in place was another matter. Just aligning the sections and getting everything joined was a very tricky process, especially the kitchen roof section, which was bit more complex than the others. But somehow we did it and throughout the dry run, the passion of the TEAM was always evident:

(Email from Gretchen LaCombe Vanicor):

I just wanted to tell you again that I truly believe we (the team) would have never made it this far without you. I will never be able to tell you how much your dedication and passion has impacted me and how much I appreciate your sacrifices. We (team+you) are all doing the very best we can and are under a lot of stress. I know I can speak for each of us when I say that the remainder of this project should really be the best part and one of the most exciting experiences of our lives.[95]

The home was finished! The decks, ramps, and plants were arrayed around the home. Furniture was put in place. We finally could step back and admire our work. It was more than we could have ever hoped. Obviously it was what we had imagined and represented in models and drawings, but it was more. It embodied our dreams, and a way of life. It was almost as if it was alive. Just as a ship is referred to as a "she" we thought of her in that way. It was time to send BeauSoleil to Washington. So it was appropriate that we have a *Bon Voyage*.

This is Louisiana and we like to throw parties. The BeauSoleil TEAM was no different. We prepared for what would be the biggest party of the whole project: the *Bon Voyage* party. Thankfully, Colleen McDaniel volunteered to plan and host the event, which was a great success. Music was provided by the stylistic jam of Pearson Cross and Terry Huval's Cajun band. Even better, we received free beer from Abita Brewing and lots of great food. Griff Blakewood, one of the most dedicated faculty volunteers, danced the night away with his wife, Alice. Before the event, we had a VIP only tour of the home, which I know wrinkled some noses because the public was dying to see the interior too. Unfortunately we could not risk any possible damage from thousands of individuals walking through the home this close to the competition. So a majority of the 500 or so in attendance could only view the home from the outside. As the culmination of *Bon Voyage*, we christened the home with champagne and symbolically sent our creation on its way with a prayer from Father Chester and short speeches by Dr. Savoie, Gretchen LaCombe Vanicor, and myself. A good time was had, but there was still much work to do.

OPPOSITE PAGE TOP LEFT
Removing Roof

OPPOSITE PAGE BOTTOM LEFT
Completed Home at Bon Voyage

ABOVE
Alice & Griff Blakewood at Bon Voyage

Greg Jefferson

STUDENT PRODUCTION ARCHITECT

Born and raised in New Orleans, Greg Jefferson grew up playing football, baseball, and all the sports that make up the magical experience of growing up in the Deep South. He got his start in sustainability at an early age when, unprompted and with no assistance, he constructed a clubhouse in his parents' backyard made of discarded materials that had been left by previous owners of the house. Not surprisingly, Jefferson naturally gravitated to the world of architecture and eventually found himself as one of team members of the BeauSoleil Home, where his prime responsibility included coordinating many of the construction documents due to his extensive AutoCAD experience.

"It was a great hands-on experience," says Jefferson. "When you're sitting behind a desk or a computer, you see things in 2D and you don't get a good grasp on what it actually takes to put something together. But by doing this project, I really believe it helped me get a greater understanding of the actual construction process. Even if it was doing something as simple as framing a door – you get a better handle on how it goes together. The project also helped us get a better understanding of our culture and how things were done back then."

HOPE:
"Hope is to believe in something that you really want to happen and to know that there's nothing that can deter you away from that."

Jefferson's favorite memories from the project are rooted in the mutual respect and camaraderie of the TEAM. "I loved hanging out with everyone at the warehouse," he says, "Even before the project was done, there was a great sense of family culture with everyone on the TEAM. It was like a family. Everyone had their own specific role and played it to the T. I'm very appreciative of all the lifelong friends I made while working on the BeauSoleil Home."

TEREX

HURRICANE / STORM PROTECTION

ISSUE

Hurricanes Katrina and Rita caused nearly $120 billion worth of damage in 2005. Insurance companies give 30% discounts for storm protection measures. Storm protection is an element of sustainability because it aids in resiliency and reduces maintanance expenditures.

BEAUSOLEIL

Hurricanes Rita and Katrina drove much of the design of the home. Steel shutters fabricated from standard 1-1/2" angles for a total of $4,767.60 ($794.60 per shutter) slide on horizontal tracks, provide protection, and resemble traditional wood shutters. SIPs panels (see SIPs sidebar) help allow for a 109 mph wind resistance and with some modifications (removing overhangs and projecting elements) could withstand up to 140 mph.

PROS

These hurricane protection measures also increase energy efficiency by creating shading and better insulated walls and roof.

CONS

Solar PV's are not storm resistant so they need to be removed in storms, covered, or if damaged, they can be replaced through insurance deductables averaging around $500.

After months of planning, design, and construction, it was finally time to pack up, disassemble the roofs, place them on the semi-trucks, and head to the competition. Without incident, the roofs were removed again and put on trailers along with the shell of the home (with a temporary roof structure and custom tarp). The two flatbed tractor-trailers left for Washington, D.C., a few days later. Our TEAM convoy consisted of a passenger van containing the driving crew towing our tool trailer, a panel van with plants, and two large Ryder trucks with all the smaller home components like decks and railings. The TEAM of 24 students and three faculty members flew out of Lafayette Regional Airport on the morning of September 28 after a send-off by the UL Lafayette Marching Band and an inspirational speech by Dr. Savoie. It would be an exciting month, with many more challenges to come as D.C. and the Solar Decathlon quickly approached.

Our flight arrived safely with no problems. However, we received word that the truck carrying the BeauSoleil home had been involved in a minor accident in a hotel parking lot. The details were fuzzy and vague; we had no idea as to the extent of the damage. Thankfully, we learned that damage

OPPOSITE PAGE
Home on its Way to D.C.

ABOVE
TEAM Leaving University

LEFT
Dr. Savoie Wishing Gjertson Good Luck

was relatively minor and cosmetic, but the episode added another layer of tension to the group. Additionally, our massive shipment of 10,000 recyclable grocery bags, was also involved in an accident and was impounded as evidence by local police. Needless to say, Father Chester's prayers were much in need on this day. Now it was time to compete.

The Competition

IT'S HARD TO IMAGINE IF YOU WERE NOT THERE. The BeauSoleil Home on Washington's National Mall is a thing to behold. It only ran for about three weeks in the fall of 2009, but what an amazing address to have while it lasted. Being adjacent to the Washington Monument and seeing the Capitol in the distance was humbling. We were honored and privileged to be on these hallowed grounds. WE WERE PRIVILEGED – we were one of only 20 universities in the world selected to complete in the 2009 Solar Decathlon.

The Solar Decathlon was conceived in the late 1990s as an initiative to highlight and promote solar energy to the public. The first competition was held in 2002 and subsequent competitions followed in 2005, 2007, 2009, 2011, and 2013 (with plans for 2015). As SolarDecathlon.org states, "The U.S. Department

of Energy Solar Decathlon is an award-winning program that challenges collegiate teams to design, build, and operate solar-powered houses that are cost-effective, energy-efficient, and attractive. The winner of the competition is the team that best blends affordability, consumer appeal, and design excellence with optimal energy production and maximum efficiency." [96] What an incredible stage for presenting alternative energy, sustainability, your state, and your university.

The Solar Decathlon has had an enormous impact not only on the public but on the participants as well. The six competitions to date have had 112 collegiate teams and have affected the lives of 17,000 student and faculty participants. In addition, the program has been expanded to include an additional 81 teams and more than 12,000 students in two spin-off competitions around the world: Solar Decathlon Europe and Solar Decathlon China.[97]

OPPOSITE PAGE
Solar Decathlon (BeauSoleil Lower Right)

ABOVE
Rain at the Solar Decathlon

An article by the *New York Times*, in which our TEAM was mentioned, had an interview with the Decathlon's founder, Richard King, where he illustrated some of the challenges of solar power and his vision for the competition:

People were slapping them (solar panels) up on roofs through the '70s and '80s, they didn't look that great. A lot of homeowner associations were saying, 'Uh, I don't want those in my neighborhood.' Because yeah, they didn't look that good... So I thought, well, let's challenge the architects to figure this out. Let's make an aesthetic house that is solar-powered and is reliable and going to work.[98]

The name "Decathlon" comes from the Olympic competition involving ten different events. Each year of the competition, the events or contests have changed slightly. In 2009, the contests were divided into five subjective contests (meaning they were judged by a jury) and five objective contests (which were determined through instrumentation/monitors in the homes.)

This extreme and demanding organization and manic comparing of apples-to-apples was both the attraction and the

2009 SOLAR DECATHLON CONTESTS

SUBJECTIVE

Architecture	evaluation of architectural elements, holistic design, and inspiration
Market Viability	evaluation of livability, constructability, and affordability
Engineering	evaluation of functionality, efficiency, innovation, and reliability
Lighting Design	evaluation of functional and aesthetic natural and artificial lighting
Communications	evaluation of team websites, communication plans, and exhibits for effectiveness

OBJECTIVE

Comfort Zone	monitoring of uniform temperature and humidity
Hot Water	monitoring of hot water temperature and volume
Appliances	monitoring of appliance energy usage
Entertainment	monitoring/scoring of ability to cook, host party, watch TV, and use as an office
Net Metering	monitoring of energy production and consumption [99]

problem with the Decathlon. There had to be tight rules, but at what point did these stifle creativity and regional-specificity? Homes should reflect their own unique local culture and climate. Also, there had been consistent criticism of the extreme cost and lack of relevance of the homes to the public. If they were over $1 million for an 800 square feet home, who could afford them?

We designed the BeauSoleil Louisiana Solar Home not for the competition, but for the people of Louisiana. However, we were about to reveal Louisiana's home to the world.

Needless to say, when the TEAM arrived in Washington on September 28, 2009, there was an elevated level of excitement and nervousness in the air. I carried a three-ring binder that was packed with logistical aspects of the trip such as: travel and transport of the team, hotel information (we had an $18,000 bill), local information such as places to get food (expenses for the TEAM totaled $23,000 in D.C..), student conduct agreements, assembly and disassembly data, and the competition rules.

After the TEAM checked into the hotel on Monday, September 28, we had two free days to get acclimated to the city. We spent these days visiting museums and seeing the local sights. Keno arrived on a flight with our students. He was a comforting presence for the TEAM, who relished his spirited personality. However, immediately upon arrival, Keno was anxious to get to work. He wasn't in Washington to vacation; he was there to work. So one of our first challenges was getting the hyper-productive Keno to relax for a day and suppress his obsessive but resolute need to always be doing something work-related. It was suggested to him that he visit some of the museums on the National Mall, which Keno did. Upon his return from the Smithsonian, Keno was awestruck and full of praise for the institution's exhibits. "Oh, I liked that museum," said Keno. "They have those bones!" Of course he was talking about the Natural History Museum with the large dinosaur displays.

At the hotel, Keno was paired to share a room with Interior Design Professor Brian Powell. Never in the history of Louisiana has there been such an odd couple; however, by all accounts the two got along well together and even bonded. In this case, bonding consisted of the mannered and erudite Powell, quietly attempting to go to bed with a sleeping mask over his face, while the rambunctious Keno slammed cans of Budweiser, brandished an imaginary pistol, and watched NASCAR races at full volume on the TV.

I shared a room with Dan Burkett. Burkett and I got along very well - passing each other on the way to our 12 hour shifts! I especially appreciated his calmness and focus that helped steady this unwieldy endeavor. Like me, Burkett had worked professionally in an architecture firm, and had construction experience that served us well. We collaborated superbly throughout the entire project.

At 11 p.m. on Wednesday, September 30, 2009, the teams were allowed to begin assembly on the National Mall. What a crazy idea! Why allow the teams to start in the middle of the night!? Apparently the National Park Service, which is in charge

Dan Burkett

ASSISTANT PROFESSOR OF ARCHITECTURE

A native of the sun-baked environs of Arizona, Dan Burkett was trained in architecture, receiving a Bachelor's degree at Arizona State University and a Master's of Architecture at Rice University. Burkett's agreeable personality, determination, and adaptability were highly valuable assets to TEAM BeauSoleil. Dan currently lives in Lafayette, Louisiana, where he practices as a designer and maker and is an assistant professor at UL Lafayette.

"We (he is married to TEAM member Kari Smith) were both excited about the project, but also a little apprehensive, because we didn't know the extent of it," says Burkett. "One of the reasons I got into it was to continue the design/build background that I had from graduate school and professionally.

"I think the intuitive design was one of the pluses we had as a team, especially with Professor Eddie Cazayoux's knowledge. Having that common sense knowledge about passive design really benefited us. It's a region specific house. My favorite part of the house is the transition space. The adaptability of it is based on the cultural recognition of how Cajun people gather. It's the BeauSoleil House; it belongs to Southern Louisiana. The team did a really good job of being true to their roots and being true to Southern Louisiana and the design parameters that are required of this region. There are some people that won't even look at sustainability. And there are others who will look at it purely financially. Some people, it's about lifestyle; some people, it's about having a lower light bill."

HOPE:
"With the students of this project, there was a great sense of hope that this project would change people. I think that was one of the biggest catalysts that got the students so heavily involved. It was the hope for change."

of the Mall, allows the Decathlon only a set number of days to operate, so the window of opportunity had to be maximized with this early start.

I remember the tension of driving out of the hotel parking lot that night in the 15-passenger van, leading the two large Ryder trucks towards the National Mall. We were an untested team, and this was our first foray into this arena. To add to this nervousness, I took a wrong turn down one of the city's labyrinthine streets and led the trucks down a smaller road under an overpass that was almost too low for the trucks to safely navigate. But somehow, we made it to the Mall. We proudly stood on these historic grounds with the Capitol lit up on one side and the Washington Monument on the other. It was an unforgettably surreal scene.

The night-time assembly crew (12 a.m. - 12 p.m.) was comprised of 12 students and faculty, including Brian Powell and I. The daytime assembly crew was also comprised of 12 students with faculty positions filled by Dan Burkett and Dr. Bob Henry. Kari Smith came to D.C. for the conclusion of the competition and the disassembly. TEAM BeauSoleil was one of the first teams to be let onto the Mall. At 11 p.m., the TEAM was given permission to drive onto the site for the BeauSoleil Home.

One of our first tasks was to find the generator and lighting in the trucks that were packed to the hilt. Somehow we located everything and started to survey and layout where the home would go. Two aspects that made this all the more difficult were that it started to rain and large plastic mats had to be laid on the grass and moved around anytime a vehicle drove on the grass. These mats were extremely heavy and slippery.

To add to this, it was cold. We did not expect D.C. in October to be so frigid. The average temperature was 49 degrees, with the low being 39 degrees.[100] One of my clearest memories was of one of my students, Trevor Ducote, who is a fairly big guy, wrapped in a blanket trying to stay warm, but still working as fast as he could.

Some time in the middle of the night, the tractor trailer carrying the BeauSoleil Home arrived. In the dark, the TEAM gingerly directed the truck back over the foundation site. Jacks were used to lift the home off of the trailer and the truck pulled away. The home, now several feet off the ground and precariously sitting on its jacks, was lowered to the correct height and placed on the adjustable steel piers. It was then leveled by

ABOVE
Night Assembly of Home

ABOVE
Assembly of Home

the ever industrious Keno using a garden hose filled with water, in the manner of the ancient Greeks who invented this self-leveling method.[101]

As the sun arose, the second tractor trailer arrived with the roof sections. The brilliance of the white National Capitol and the Washington Monument glowing in the morning sun was breathtaking. All of a sudden, as we were working, we heard applause. We turned to see that the daytime assembly crew had arrived early for their shift at 10 a.m. Their enthusiasm and support sent a bolt of warmth and pride through us as we plodded home on the Metro for a well deserved day of sleep. The daytime crew then placed the roofs on the home with a rented crane. On October 2, the nighttime crew installed the bump-outs (shower and washer/dryer modules) and started to layout the exterior decks. Shortly after, the daytime crew started the PV and deck installations.

The alternating shifts went on for four days. The demands of each 12-hour shift took a toll on the TEAM, but all found the inner strength to rally when needed. Somehow we assembled everything, and I drove with Denisse Castro Dufreche, Chris Dufreche, and Theresa Guidry to get the plants and vegetation, which were stored at a home outside of D.C. There was limited space to store material on the Mall, so we stored many of our things off-site at the hotel, in our trucks, or at whatever improvised location we could find.

Theresa, or Ms. T as we called her, was a Master Gardener and a dedicated volunteer who stayed with us from the early design stage through the competition. Ms. T was a life-saver in terms of keeping the plants healthy and getting them in place. But she was also wise – offering advice and counseling to the students on all matters. The landscaping was a prolific and vibrant demonstration of the various biomes (distinct landscape environments) of Louisiana.[102] Roy Dufreche, the father of Chris Dufreche, was our landscape architect. He worked closely

Denisse Castro Dufreche

INSTRUMENTATION OFFICER

Born and raised in Matanzas, Cuba, until the age of 10, Denise Castro and her family migrated to the United States and settled in New Orleans. During her years in Cuba, she grew up in the lush habitat of the northern shore with fruits, vegetables, and coffee, mango, avocado, and guava trees growing in abundance around her. As the Instrumentation Officer, Castro's high energy, diligence, and assertiveness served as major assets of TEAM BeauSoleil.

"I was given the title of Instrumentation Officer, which primarily involved getting the home ready for all of the testing," says Castro. "What I really enjoyed was taking part in the design development and watching our ideas come into reality all the way from our first basswood model. As the design progressed I took on the exterior porch design along with the entry ramp and landscape. Really, just working on the construction documents set was fun and rewarding.

"There were many rewards. All of us grew so much from this project, not just as designers, but also as individuals. Just being able to see a project all the way through while still in school was an amazing experience that cannot be compared to anything else architecture students experience. It taught me to look at a project as a whole and not just one small part. It also taught me how challenging working with a group can be. It also taught me that there is not one right solution to a problem; there are always multiple ones; we just have to be open to the possibilities."

HOPE:
"Hope is that our generation will be the leaders in promoting a tangible sustainable architecture throughout the world."

Theresa D. Guidry (Ms. T)

MASTER GARDENER

One of 12 children, Theresa "Ms. T" Guidry grew up on North Sterling Street in upper Lafayette, Louisiana, where her father was one of the first (if not the first) plastering contractors in the city. He was instrumental in the construction of the University of Louisiana at Lafayette (then known as USL) campus. Ms. T's enthusiastic and motherly presence was another much appreciated personality on TEAM BeauSoleil. With her master gardening skills, she was responsible for keeping the real "green" in the project, the plants, alive.

"We were always taught to give, to help each other," says Ms. T. "My mother and father were very optimistic people, so being part of TEAM BeauSoleil was one of my greatest rewards. There was no hesitation when I was asked to be part of the project. My husband and I love to give back. I really enjoyed the experience, but it was a lot of work. We had to grow everything at home and transport it to Washington, D.C., which creates its own problems

"For the BeauSoleil Home, I used a lot of vegetables and container gardens, because that's what I do; I teach container gardening. I was just a little tiny part of it, but I loved working with these kids; they respected me, and they trusted me. Also, I absolutely loved the landscape design that landscape architect Roy Dufreche came up with. Another thing I noticed was a lot of the students from other universities at the Solar Decathlon did not have that same energy, enthusiasm, and drive that these kids from UL Lafayette had."

HOPE:
"Hope is a feeling that what is wanted...will happen."

with nurseries in the Hammond area, our student officer Denisse Castro Dufreche, and with Ms. T to design and implement a landscape environment that was beautifully representative of Louisiana and the BeauSoleil Home.

ABOVE
Kitchen Herb Garden

One thing that I had not really taken into consideration was food and water supplies for the TEAM when assembling the home, especially at night when most stores were closed. During the day the organizers provided some meals. Thankfully, Colleen McDaniel arranged for coffee to be delivered in the middle of the night to us from a delivery service. I have no idea what the cost of this was, but it's another profound example of McDaniel's nurturing of the TEAM. It was also a unique opportunity for the TEAM to meet some of the other teams, such as the Germans, who upon smelling our coffee, approached to ask us where we got it. We had a few extra cups, so we graciously passed them on to the highly organized but fairly reserved Germans, whose house (which went on to win the whole competition) had the unusual quality of resembling a black Rubik's cube. Sharing coffee made the competition seem more intimate.

Luckily our hotel provided dinner and breakfast as well as kitchens within our rooms.[103] These small but important details made our one-month stay much more agreeable. Even though the hotel was located across the Potomac River from the National Mall, it was immediately next to a Metro station so the commute back and forth was relatively easy. It must have been a strange sight for D.C. commuters to see us coming and going each day, covered in dirt and sweat, in TEAM uniforms and hardhats. McDaniel and I got groceries for the TEAM on one or two occasions, but for the most part, the TEAM members fended for themselves. And although the students were responsible adults, we had a policy in place that prevented anyone - faculty or students on the TEAM - from drinking alcohol within six hours of their work shift.

In the final hours leading up to the start of the competition, we secured our building inspection. It required a thorough bit of back and forth with the code official with whom we negotiated. Much of it dealt with ramp transitions, stairs, railings, and other details that could affect access by the public. One of the last things to get approved was the electrical inspection

Colleen McDaniel

TEAM MOM

Dubbed the "mom" of the team, Colleen McDaniel is also the actual mother of Student Project Architect Scott Chappuis. When the team needed food, coffee, or some other form of assistance, the Lafayette, Louisiana-born McDaniel was there to provide it. Few will dispute the fact that she gave priceless emotional support for all those involved as well. In addition, she orchestrated the *Bon Voyage* party for the TEAM and made the trip with them to the Solar Decathlon, assisting in various capacities wherever she was needed.

"I saw everyone working on the BeauSoleil Home in the warehouse and thought, 'Who is going to take care of those kids?' That's how I got involved," says McDaniel. "I was in way over my head with the *Bon Voyage* party, but I got a friend of mine involved and she helped me out a great deal. If I had to do it again, I would've engaged caterers to bring food."

HOPE:
"Hope is the belief that tomorrow will be better than today."

Like many of the others involved with BeauSoleil Home, the upbringing McDaniel experienced in Louisiana prepped her for this project in sustainability. "When I was growing up, my father didn't want us wasting anything," says McDaniel. "Close the doors. Close the refrigerator. I guess it was economy driven, rather than ecologically driven when I grew up. The BeauSoleil Home made me more aware about environmental issues. In the future, I'd want a house with solar components and some of the new things with energy savings and efficiency. Every appliance I've bought since the project, I try to make sure it's more energy efficient. For me, it's a spiritual thing. We were put here to steward the earth. And if we do the opposite, we're not fulfilling what God wants us to do."

and grid interconnect permit. This was the responsibility of the electrical team and I deferred to them. The electrical team consisted of five people: Dr. Henry, William Depa, David Carroll, Marsela Jakob-Wood (seniors), and Christian DePrins.

The electrical inspection occurred on the evening before the competition. At the same time, there was a dinner reception for faculty advisers at the Smithsonian. I felt confident that the TEAM would get the electrical issues worked out and the permit granted so I decided to attend the dinner. Not long after arriving at the reception, I got a call from someone on the TEAM, saying they were having trouble. I didn't think I could do anything to remedy the situation. It turned out the L.E.D. low-voltage transformers were tripping circuit breakers and thus we were having trouble passing inspection. In the last few minutes before the deadline, someone ran to another team's house and borrowed some extra electrical outlets which were used to replace our GFIC breaker outlets. This did the trick.

ABOVE
Inspectors in Kitchen

Vanicor posted a recap of that night's events which got picked-up by the *New York Times*:[104]

WE PASSED! WE PASSED! WE PASSED!

WOW!!! What an amazing day for TEAM BeauSoleil! WE pulled it all together and passed all of our inspections with only minutes to spare...

Tonight, I witnessed the most incredible teamwork I have EVER seen. It was absolutely inspiring. WE worked together, kept our cool, and solved the problem. This is part of what makes our TEAM so special. We ALL truly believe in what we are doing and are extremely proud to represent our University, our culture, and our state.

I would like to thank Ms. T, Mrs. Billie (Henry), Father Chester, and everyone back home who were praying for us (I really think this helped us through) and our incredible faculty members for helping us solve this problem. Also, we owe a huge amount of gratitude to the other Solar Decathlon teams (TEAM Missouri, The University of Arizona, The Ohio State University, University of Kentucky, and Universidad de Puerto Rico) who were so kind to help us out. We truly could not have done it without you! [105]

ABOVE
Home Open for Tours in the Rain

RIGHT
Opening Ceremony (TEAM Lower Right)

Later that evening and into the next day, I felt terrible I had not been there in this moment of crisis. In fact, to this day, I still feel guilty. No one has ever said that I should have been there, but I still wonder, five years later, if the students hold this against me. The magnitude and weight of the competition induced both great pride and guilt at times. But in D.C., there was no time to cry over spilled milk.

The opening day of the Solar Decathlon competition was amazing. There was a palpable energy in the air that surrounded all the teams as they made minor adjustments on their houses and hustled about the historic lawn of the National Mall. After TEAM BeauSoleil posed for a group photo with all

David Carroll

STUDENT ELECTRICAL ENGINEER

Born and raised in Lafayette, David Carroll studied electrical engineering at UL Lafayette. Like many of the other students, he had a very active childhood, playing a variety of sports and spending quality time outdoors. Carroll, who has worked at a professional engineering firm since 2007, was another ideal candidate for participation in the BeauSoleil Home. He now works as an electrical designer and project manager.

HOPE: "Hope is positivity, which is essential for a prosperous future."

"I was one of three members of the electrical senior design team," says Carroll. "It was our senior design project to design and install the solar photovoltaic system for the house. As part of the design project, we documented and analyzed the performance of the system before and during the Solar Decathlon competition. We also aided in constructing the home here in Lafayette and deconstructing it for preparation to ship to Washington, D.C. There, I was on the night shift team to put the home back together, re-install the solar photovoltaic system, and prepare the home for the competition. The long hours of the night shift and adjusting to the sleep schedule were difficult.

"It was a very unique and exciting project and competition. I most enjoyed being on the National Mall, sandwiched right between the U.S. Capitol and the Washington Monument. It was very surreal to be constructing houses on this landmark.

"The Solar Decathlon competition is a great way to get students involved in green technology and sustainability. It inspires them to pursue careers in the energy conservation industry. And it brings awareness to those who do not know much about green technology and sustainability. I believe it is important for everyone to be educated on the subject of energy conservation, and it is . . . projects like this, that help spread that knowledge."

TOP
View Out of Bedroom

ABOVE
Dr. Savoie Helping with Plants

OPPOSITE PAGE
Celebrating Market Viability Win

the other teams, we ran back to our site for the ribbon-cutting and a blessing by Father Chester. Lines of people began to form. The tours began minutes later. There was no time to catch our breath.

Later, in a moment of reflection, I jotted-down my amazement at just being in Washington on the National Mall. After all, no one looks out their bedroom window and sees the unobstructed Capitol dome straight ahead!

What an incredible view! This is a one of a kind view we will never have again...We had our architecture, market viability and communication's juries today...There were multiple "wows!" from the market viability jury when they saw our kitchen and bathroom! Sarah Susanka, on the architecture jury, said she loved our herb wall and wanted to use the idea in one of her projects! She was snapping pictures like crazy in our home.

We were also honored with the presence of Dr. Joseph Savoie for the last two days. President Savoie even helped pick up trash and arrange our water plants. Our President is truly "hands-on" and more importantly, he cares deeply about our students.[106]

THE WINNERS OF THE FIRST SET OF JURIED/SUBJECTIVE contests were to be announced on the fifth day of the competition, October 12. The student officers and I gathered in the cold in front of the podium. The first award was the Architecture Award. The TEAM was disappointed that we did not fall in the top three

MARKET VIABILITY CONTEST CRITERIA

LIVABILITY - How well the home fits the specific needs of a targeted homeowner and whether it is a safe, comfortable, and convenient place to live,

BUILDABILITY - Whether the home can be built efficiently at a cost-competitive price and constructed the way the team intended it to be built, and

MARKETABILITY - How well the house's curb appeal, interior appeal, quality craftsmanship, as well as its sustainability features and integration of solar technology, offer potential homebuyers a good value.[108]

as we believed we would based upon the jury comments. Next the Market Viability contest was announced. At 10:53 a.m., the announcer read the winner and it became clear, halfway through his announcement, that BeauSoleil had won when the words *joie de vivre,* were read! True, unadulterated elation ensued.

The Organizers released this statement about the judging:

"The (BeauSoleil) house hit on all cylinders," said Joyce Mason, Market Viability judge and vice president for marketing with Pardee Homes. "We were so impressed with the degree to which the team listened to their market. They didn't impose their ideas or try to infer them upon their residents." [107]

Ms. Mason hit it right on the head, we never imposed our ideas. We tried to beautifully accommodate the needs and desires of our market - the people of Louisiana. Specifically, the jury considered the livability, buildability, and marketability and found the BeauSoleil Home the winner. TEAM BeauSoleil scored 97 out of 100 possible points.

The moment when the TEAM won the Market Viability contest was, for many, validation of all we had set out to do - design a culturally and climatically relevant home for our people. As Gretchen LaCombe Vanicor said in the BeauSoleil Blog, "We paid a lot of attention to what our culture is all about - our

Colin Gould

STUDENT MECHANICAL ENGINEER

Son of TEAM BeauSoleil's photographer Philip Gould, Colin Gould was one of the few mechanical engineering students to get involved with the project and stay from beginning to end. Born in Lafayette, he grew up in the country, surrounded by nature, where he lived in a house built by his grandfather. Gould's dedicated work ethic, tenacity, and methodical intelligence were invaluable assets to the project and the cohesive nature of the TEAM.

"I was just looking for a project to work on," says Gould. "I really didn't know the scope of it, but I joined on. The majority of the conceptual ownership of the project was with the architecture department and faculty, but the technological scope of the project was enough to interest engineers. Growing up in a family that was a little more progressive, and perhaps liberal, may have influenced my getting involved.

"I was in charge of the solar water heater. We had 10 minutes to get 15 gallons of water to 110 degrees Fahrenheit. Previously, we'd gotten the temperature up to 140 degrees, so that was no problem. But at the competition, in the allotted 10 minutes, we couldn't get the proper water flow... simply because the pipe in the on-demand electric hot water heater was too small. That was an oversight that nobody really knew to check. So we lost big on that...even though our hot water heater worked in principle. Everything was designed well and worked.

"Some of the houses in the competition were very heavy on technology. You'd open up the back walls to them and it was just full of technology, whereas ours was a little more integrated and subtle, which may have been a good thing, because it made the house look better. The comment that was most heard at the competition was that the BeauSoleil Home was the house the people would most want to live in."

HOPE:
"Hope is showing that you can live in a really nice place, but without such high demands for energy and space."

ABOVE
Tour Line in the Rain

climate, our kitchen. We knew from the beginning we had to make this home for the people of Acadiana and Louisiana."

In a way, none of the other contests mattered. Market Viability was the jewel. And it's a good thing that Market Viability meant so much to our TEAM, because in short order everything went downhill. First off, it began to rain. Thus, our home was not able to generate solar energy, which obviously was the main focus of the Decathlon. Of course all of the teams' homes were experiencing this same condition but we also had other problems. It's funny how you don't realize how much you depend on something until it's gone.

We discovered, the hard way, that hot water generation is one of the biggest consumers of energy. We soon found ourselves confronted with this challenge. Through testing, it was revealed that our back-up electric water heater could not keep up with the volume demand for the hot water contest. Because of the overcast rainy conditions, the home was not efficient enough or energy positive enough (it was barely energy neutral), to compensate.

The hot water heating debacle proved to be our Achilles' heel. In some ways it should be the most basic and easy system to engineer and operate. However, past Decathlon schools such as the University of Texas had warned us that these systems were difficult to move, set-up, and operate. As Professor Cazayoux addressed in the Foreword, the TEAM had made the choice to design and build a custom flat plate collector. And although this was difficult to build, it was not the ultimate problem with our system. The system had been tested by Colin Gould on October 8, 2009, the day the competition began, and it produced 140 degree water, which was more than adequate for the hot water contest. Gould was the sole mechanical engineering student and did extremely well under the circumstances.

ABOVE

Bedroom, Kitchen, and Living Room

OPPOSITE PAGE

Durio Giving Tour of Kitchen

However, we did not have the sun. So, our supposedly high-powered German instantaneous electric back-up water heater was therefore tasked to fill the demand. But it could not keep up with the daily draws of 15 gallons of 110 degree water. It was a complete mystery at the time, but we eventually discovered the reason why: the small diameter tubing in the unit was inadequate to provide the volume and rate needed in the competition, especially when the test coincided with washing clothes and dishes simultaneously.

By this point in the competition, our plumber, Robert Bergeron, from Ville Platte, and Colin Gould had already returned to Louisiana. The TEAM was without any water system specialists. On Sunday, October 11, I started calling plumbers in the D.C. yellow pages. Have you ever tried to get a plumber on a Sunday to make a house-call to the National Mall!? The TEAM paid heavily for this service. Over the next few days, the new plumber replaced the instantaneous water heater with a small tank heater.

The TEAM passed several hot water draws but our fate was sealed. Not only did we end up at the bottom of the hot water contest standings, but because of the extra energy used trying to correct the water heating situation (and the extravagant dinner contests! [see below]) and the ongoing rain, the BeauSoleil Home was one of five homes which consumed more energy than it produced at the 2009 Solar Decathlon.[109]

The Home Entertainment Contest was one which the TEAM expected to win without problem. After all, we had Cajun cooking and hospitality! The contest required each team to invite six guests from the neighboring teams (Arizona and Wisconsin) over for dinner and a movie on two occasions. Then the visiting team would score the other and vice versa. Just as we had not had time to practice the hot water draws or operation of the home, we had not practiced making dinner

either! And just like stubborn Cajuns who place a high value on fresh home-cooked food, my students would not settle for pre-prepared food or food made by someone else off site or even food heated in a microwave!

Of course none of these foods were chosen because they could be cooked quickly and utilize less energy. They were elaborate, heat-generating dishes. Our electrical engineering professor, Dr. Henry, mildly reprimanded the student TEAM for wasting so much energy. But the students would have it no other way. There was no way they would cook something un-Cajun!

Before TEAM BeauSoleil left Lafayette, the University contracted with a media services company to help cover the

DINNER SERVED BY TEAM BEAUSOLEIL

STARTER

Boiled shrimp with cocktail sauce

ENTRÉE

Seafood stuffed tilapia with a Cajun lemon butter sauce

SIDES

Garlic mashed potatoes

Green beans with bacon

DESSERT

Traditional Louisiana bread pudding with white chocolate sauce[110]

RIGHT

Vanicor Giving Tour of Dogtrot

BELOW

Accepting People's Choice Award

exploits in D.C. and promote the University. Their support obviously helped get the word out for the People's Choice award. Unofficially, we received approximately 17,000 votes, making the BeauSoleil Home the overall winner. Many of the votes were texted in from our distant supporters. Although we had done poorly in the second half of the competition, this win helped lift our spirits. As Charles Kramer, one of my good friends from childhood texted: "I veauxted!"[111]

Many, many family, friends, alumni, and supporters came to Washington, D.C., for the Solar Decathlon. It was so humbling to have that kind of turn-out. There were over 300,000 total visitors on the Mall over the course of the competition. There is no way to determine the exact number, but I estimate that there were over 1,000 from Louisiana. This included many faculty and students from our School – the 2nd, 3rd, and 4th year architecture classes. And the tours were relentless. We had 17,403 visitors in our home – 2,684 on one day! We also discovered that we had an active and robust alumni association in the D.C. area. They not only donated quite a bit of money for the project, but they also served gumbo to us one night in Washington – a comforting taste of home.

A favorite memory of many from the competition was that of our University President, Dr. E. Joseph Savoie, who made the trip to D.C. and assisted the TEAM on several notable occasions. In one instance, he and Father Chester actually carried buckets of water from the Smithsonian to the

Dr. E. Joseph Savoie

UL LAFAYETTE PRESIDENT

The fifth of seven children, Dr. E. Joseph Savoie (or "T-Joe" as he is known to many), was born in the blue-collar environs of Sulphur, Louisiana. His mother was a school teacher, and his father was a businessman. A natural leader and hard worker, Dr. Savoie became the University of Louisiana at Lafayette's sixth president in 2008.

He previously served as Louisiana's Commissioner of Higher Education for 12 years. Under his leadership, higher education governance in Louisiana was restructured, a statewide community and technical college system was created, teacher education programs were redesigned, and a master plan for public postsecondary education was implemented.

Dr. Savoie holds a doctorate in educational leadership from Columbia University's Teacher's College in New York. He earned bachelor's and master's degrees from UL Lafayette, where he became the University's first vice president for University Advancement in 1992.

From the very beginning of the project, Savoie championed the BeauSoleil Home, monitoring various stages of its design and construction; moreover, he attended the Solar Decathlon in Washington, D.C., with the TEAM. Never one to stand around and do nothing, Savoie even assisted the TEAM during heated stages of the competition.

"When I think of the BeauSoleil Home, the idea of pride comes to mind – pride from UL Lafayette being put on the international stage and pride in all the students who participated. And lastly, pride in the community who rallied to support this project," says Savoie.

HOPE:
"Hope is the sense that the work you are doing will result in something being better. You have to have the hope that things can improve."

"It was a bold project, because the home was entered into an international competition. But it was the right time to do something like that. And the enthusiasm overcame any trepidation about stepping on that stage. When you see something that gets everyone that excited – the commitment of the students – it's hard not to support. People get excited when young people are passionate about something. It was encouraging for me; because that is the kind of commitment and enthusiasm you want to see in students.

"In addition, many local businesses, and people outside the project, donated their time and resources. It's kind of like sports in that it created the same kind of emotional commitment from people. I was glad to be a part of it. It showed that we can compete in this arena on the world stage. And it spurred on this sustainability effort and made people more sensitive to it. All of those are good, positive, long term results. And I'm sure the students learned many life lessons that will stay with them forever as a result of this project."

BeauSoleil Home for Ms. T's plants: Savoie in his suit and Father Chester in his cassock. The security guard who stopped them during their trek must have been extremely confused. "A priest and a man in suit carrying buckets of water..."- it sounds like the opening line to a joke! We couldn't have asked for a better supporter than "T-Joe" Savoie, a man who truly cared about his students, school, and home state.

On October 16 at 5 p.m., Michael Doucet and the band BeauSoleil arrived. They finally got to see the home with their name. They loved it. Unfortunately it was cold and rainy so they set up in the main tent. This was unprecedented. No other Decathlon team had ever brought their own band to perform. The Decathlon organizers, especially, Richard King (the DoE Director of the Decathlon) were elated. He and his wife danced the night away. It was a bit strange at first. BeauSoleil started playing and everyone stood around the perimeter watching awkwardly. Finally, one of our students went to the center and started dancing. Eventually everyone was dancing! I had one of several reunions with my family at the competition, and I finally started to relax and bask in the glow of success and relief. In a way though, the entire competition was a blur to me. Too much was happening, and I continue to meet people who were there that I don't even remember seeing. Someone said that it was like your own wedding where so much was happening it was like a dream.

TOP
BeauSoleil avec Michael Doucet

ABOVE
Hector LaSala Dancing

OPPOSITE
Packing Up in D.C.

Upon completion of the competition, it was time to pack up and go home. This was a bittersweet moment. We were winners and losers. Our best four contests were Market Viability (1st), Appliances (6th), Comfort Zone (7th), and Home Entertainment (7th), but we had scored second to last overall.[112] Of course First in People's Choice was a saving grace. We were exhausted, and now we had to safely dismantle the home, take it back to Louisiana, and put it back together. It would be a long road home, but a satisfying and accomplished one.

The last moment where I exerted my authority and got in a brief verbal war with my students was on our last day in D.C., when the house was about to be loaded on a flat-bed truck.

The house was being jacked up several feet above the ground and some temporary shoring was being put in place. When we initially placed the house on the site, we were much more deliberate and careful: we were working in unison, communicating, and putting in lots of temporary shoring in the form of concrete blocks. Keno was with us at this point. His presence lent an air of authority, experience, and calm to the process. But at this point, Keno was gone and everyone was tired and ready to go home. I remember Michael Garrison from the 2005 and 2007 UT team saying, "make sure you have a fresh team of students for disassembly." I should have listened to him. We did have three or four new students, but we really needed more. Our team officers were physically and emotionally exhausted and ready to go home.

At some point I realized we were in an unsafe situation. I told everyone to stop and back away and several of us went to get more concrete blocks from other teams. I probably over compensated in some sense, because if anything, I was self-conscious that I was not concerned enough about safety at all times. But here we were - almost done and on the home stretch. I didn't want anything to happen now. I'm glad I did it even though it was unpleasant at the time. We safely loaded the house onto the flatbed truck and all was well. It was time to call it a day.

On October 21, we left D.C. Most of the TEAM flew back to Lafayette, where they were greeted by Ken Ardoin, families, and other university supporters waving signs at the Lafayette airport. The next day, Chris Leger, Greg Jefferson, Chris Dufreche, Denisse Castro Dufreche, Ms. T, and I drove the van and the trucks home, which was not without its share of drama. Somewhere in Virginia, the tarp started to come off the roof sections. We had to stop and hastily reattach it. I also gave members of the TEAM a rousing wake-up call when I accidentally down-shifted the passenger van into PARK while traveling at 60 MPH. The van was not hurt, but I like to think that the horrendous grind of the transmission, which made an ungodly racket, served as a clarion call to slow down and take things one day at a time.

The caravan TEAM finally made it home on October 22 to little fanfare since the rest of the TEAM had already arrived by airplane. The best greeting was from my family, however. Their love and patience over the entire two year endeavor was what got me through it. That weekend we rode in the UL Lafayette Homecoming parade (with my daughters Elise and Alex) as victors and were given the opportunity to walk onto the football field at halftime to uproarious applause. It was extremely gratifying.

But there was no rest for the weary. On the following Monday, we began unpacking and reorganizing our cargo. We utilized the entire School to unpack the trucks and placed much of it in a shipping container. We had decided just prior to the competition that the home would be relocated to our campus adjacent to the architecture building. Director McKinney and the physical plant worked out the details while we were in D.C.

ABOVE
Home on Campus in Lafayette

OPPOSITE PAGE TOP
Homecoming Parade

OPPOSITE PAGE BOTTOM
People's Choice Award

The home arrived in Baton Rouge, Louisiana, a few days later, and the following week, it was delivered to the UL Lafayette campus where we had prepared concrete foundation pads. Putting the home in place proved quite problematic due to the high street curbs and muddy ground in the area. After the flatbed truck got stuck and eventually pulled free with a tow-truck, we began making real progress toward the reassembly.[113] The crane arrived a day later and we reattached the roof. The remaining set-up and start-up took several weeks and required many hours to properly accomplish. After completing these tasks, the TEAM was exhausted and probably in need of a good long break, free from anything BeauSoleil-related. However, not long after, the governor's wife, Supriya Jindal, toured the BeauSoleil Home and presented each of us with a

commemorative, official pin. Although this was an honor it was difficult to get up the energy for yet another event!

December and the winter break could not have come soon enough. We all desperately needed rest. The TEAM had done their job. And the job was done. I could not ask them to do any more. It was an amazing journey, and I am infinitely proud to have made it with them. Even now, when work needs to be done on the BeauSoleil Home, I cannot ask the primary TEAM officers. They gave it their all. This is often just a cliché – but not in this case. I'm truly proud of each and every member of our TEAM. They showed courage and spirit when it was needed. They showed strength of character when it was in short supply. They showed resiliency and determined resolve when all were past the point of exhaustion.

Afterward, I continued to feel the obligations to our University, the UL Lafayette administration, our community, and our partners. I put together thank-you notes and CDs with images over the Christmas break to send to all of them. I also produced a small picture book called, *through the thicket: The BeauSoleil Louisiana Solar Home* on blurb.com. The title *through the thicket* comes from something supposedly attributed to Louis Kahn, my favorite architect. Kahn talked about the difficulty of taking an idea from conception to a built work. He spoke of how when going "through the thicket," everything is tugging and ripping at you and your design to try to compromise it.[114] But the design must remain intact. This is what I felt we had done. We had designed a culturally and climatically relevant home

ABOVE
Home on Campus in Lafayette

for Louisiana AND we had won Market-Viability and People's Choice. We had our cake and ate it too.

One of our big supporters, internationally recognized architect and founder of Architecture 2030 Ed Mazria, summed it up nicely in an email to Eddie Cazayoux: "Congratulations on both MV (market viability) first place and the People's Choice Award. We need examples of good region specific designs that can be replicated and marketed so we can get on with addressing the critical issues of our time – before it's too late."[115]

Solar energy is modern alchemy. Just as the alchemists tried to convert base metals to gold, a photovoltaic cell converts photons from the sun to electrons. Money for nothing. What could be more attractive?

When we were designing and building the BeauSoleil Home, we always spoke of it as a hybrid, much like the Toyota Prius. The BeauSoleil Home was designed to break into the market for solar homes. The BeauSoleil Home tried to sell solar, make it marketable, and help everyone transition to greater self-sufficiency. It was not completely self-sufficient (although our film made it sound like that) but connected to the grid while still producing most of its own power. Just as most people are not willing to completely give up gas and go all-electric with their cars, most people are not ready to go off-the-grid with their homes.

What I've come to realize is that the BeauSoleil Home was in the right place at the right time to begin a conversation about self-sufficiency, conservation, and alternative energy. It was non-threatening to most people (although our film did begin with doom and gloom.) It was non-hippie – it didn't espouse alternative lifestyles or outrageous haircuts and bolts through noses. We were apolitical. It was about building responsibly. It was about building smart. It was about building strong. This was especially relevant after hurricanes Katrina and Rita. It was about maintaining a low center of gravity while cultivating a high understanding of our natural environment.

Truth be told, almost nothing can be completely sustainable. But it does not hurt to try to improve our lives in productive ways that curtail mindless consumption. There are tradeoffs, and there has to be a balance. Whether we like it or not, our presence here on earth in ever-increasing numbers is consuming our resources and degrading our environment. It's hard to imagine a day when every building has a net zero energy/carbon footprint. It's hard to imagine every person producing more than they consume. It is an insurmountable problem.

But the success of BeauSoleil was that we were trying... and we were trying extremely hard. And we made the process and product fun and inclusive. We made it easier for people to adopt sustainability – not easy, but easier. We tried to make it somewhat convenient to be green. We tried to show that severe sacrifices did not have to be made to be green. And we tried to show that although lifestyle changes would be required to live in the BeauSoleil home, they were enjoyable and it would improve the quality of life.

Was it worth $800,000? (The project cost about $400,000 in cash and $400,000 in in-kind services/goods. The home itself was about $300,000.) Is this not as excessive and wasteful as what we were fighting against? Even though the project required an enormous expenditure of resources, it was worth it. And I have yet to hear any argument to the contrary. We had a huge impact and got the word out on a regional and national stage. But, we were under no green illusions.[116] We knew we were not going to change the world. But by creating the BeauSoleil Home we could usher in a community and region-wide dialogue about building responsibly. And with that, maybe we could actually generate hope for our future and that of others.

AFTERWORD

sounds, touches,
tastes and smells of
home. As time passes and
the sun comes around to
face the home, you

The BeauSoleil Home Today

THE BEAUSOLEIL HOME SERVES MANY INTERests today on the campus of the University of Louisiana at Lafayette (it is connected by its own short sidewalk just one minute from the art, architecture, and design building.) First, the home is a trophy - a reminder of our wins at the 2009 Solar Decathlon. It is also a classroom - successive generations of students visit the home every year to learn about sustainable design. The BeauSoleil Home represents ongoing applied research. The performance of the systems and the livability of the home continue to be tested and monitored.

Next, the BeauSoleil Home is a university facility and is used for events such as orientation day, faculty meetings, and even office space from time to time. It is a bed and breakfast - university guests can stay for a night and enjoy its features and comforts.

Finally, the BeauSoleil home is an example - a tangible example - of smart, sustainable housing. It is an example to the students and the community. And it is a prototype for other houses built by the School of Architecture and Design's Building Institute. We also continue to hope that it will become a prototype for a version that can be produced in large volume. I don't like the word "mass-produced." I would hate to see 3,000 exact copies side by side. But certainly, the BeauSoleil Home should be produced in great numbers with various configurations and options. There is still an enormous need for affordable and sustainable housing like BeauSoleil.

The BeauSoleil Home has been reassembled and operational since November 30, 2009. It has been almost continuously utilized with weekly tours for the public, classes, conferences, presentations, and overnight stays by members of the faculty, students, and the public. We also continue to do public outreach, receive awards, and make presentations to various civic and educational groups. During the Spring 2010 semester, the TEAM's student officers finished thesis projects that researched various aspects of the BeauSoleil Home, like passive thermal performance, mass-customization, social responsibility, marketing of sustainability, urban adaptation, cultural responsiveness, landscape, and the philosophy of sustainability. The students even held their final presentations in the home. Imagine that, actually building your thesis project. And then, presenting inside it.

The home continues to be acclimated to its site and the finishing touches continue to be added - for example, landscaping, an irrigation system, gutters and downspouts connected to the cistern, and awnings over the windows on the south side. I kept my office in the home for the first year after the competition in order to keep it open for tours.

A senior project team from the College of Engineering analyzed the problems from the hot water system and made upgrades in 2011, and other engineering teams installed monitoring instruments to record energy consumption and production in 2012. Now anyone can check the energy generation and usage on the real-time energy dashboard for the BeauSoleil Home: http://egauge1919.egaugegaug.es/kiosk/.

The home was officially dedicated on its new campus site on March 25, 2010. It was an opportunity to thank the hundreds of TEAM members and sponsors. A beautiful stainless steel plaque mounted near the entrance to the home recognizes them. We received a generous donation soon after the dedication from the Louisiana Contractor's Educational Trust Fund, which allows for continual educational programs.

We let students who worked on the project stay overnight in the home, and we began auctioning off nights for *Festivals Acadiens et Créoles* (located in the park across the street from the home) to raise money for the College, Alumni Center, and Our Lady of Wisdom. Over 40 guests have stayed in the home. From the first year, when we had an average of 2 or 3 visitors to the home per week, it has leveled off to about one on average per week. We don't have a definite number, but based on this estimate and the records of the visitors at the competition, tours, and events we have had over 20,000 visitors to the BeauSoleil home through 2014.

"Thanks to Geoff and all of the students who put so much work and thought into the project, and to UL and the many generous sponsors who believed in it.

The home is very comfortable, livable and user-friendly. John and I look forward to continued efforts to bring solar and other forms of renewable energy to all."

COLLEEN MCDANIEL CHAPPUIS

Just like in a bed and breakfast, we ask overnight guests to record their comments in a guest book. Megan Durio, one of the student TEAM members stated, "I don't want to go. I had an amazing time here in the house. Couldn't ask for better weather. Never used the AC power! I feel so lucky to be able to have stayed here for the weekend."[117] Another said, "Hate saying goodbye to this house."[118] The only criticism seems to be that curious bystanders often peep into the home not knowing that there are guests staying there!

In 2010, the University trademarked the BeauSoleil Home name and logo and developed a licensing agreement should a manufacturer or owner want to replicate the home. We are still searching for a modular home manufacturer to build the home. Unfortunately, the economy has been so poor that no company had been interested. We also established a system whereby a homeowner can license the trademark and hire one of the BeauSoleil TEAM alumni to work with them to develop the home design for their property, produce plans, and observe construction. So far, although many have started the process, none have completed a BeauSoleil Home Version Two.

In 2011, Liz Landry from the President's Office contacted me about starting a Campus Office of Sustainability. The University Strategic Plan, guided by the wisdom of the President, emphasized sustainability. We agreed to let the BeauSoleil Home be the headquarters. How appropriate – the Home for Sustainability. For two years, a graduate student director, Laura Bullinger, worked out of the home and in 2013, Gretchen LaCombe Vanicor, the BeauSoleil Project Manager, was selected in a national search as UL Lafayette's first Director of Sustainability. Vanicor reports directly to the President and is charged with developing and implementing the University's Sustainability Policy and Plan. Vanicor's position is a prime example of the impact and significance of the BeauSoleil Home.

Every year or so, we have a BeauSoleil Home spring cleaning. Like any state facility, ongoing maintenance is an issue. We continue to consider the possibility of a new site for the home. Lafayette's new Central Park (the Horse Farm) may yet still be the best place for it. I still consider the home my baby, and I only want the best for her. Just like parents putting up a baby for adoption because they know they cannot care for it, I would be willing to see her go if she will be utilized and cared for better than on our campus. However, 69% of the public and students support the home staying on the UL Lafayette campus.[119]

So what's in the future for the BeauSoleil Louisiana Solar Home? We will continue to look at the possibility of mass-producing a version of the BeauSoleil Home. What are the reasons for this failure to build a mass-produced version? From our public survey the biggest impediments are: cost (29%) and the lack of modular home industry support (20%). However, when asked what needed to be changed, the small size (30%) was more important than the cost (24%).[120]

At minimum we hope to find a few individuals who would like to build one for themselves. This replication would allow the University to study the production model and gain valuable insight and research. We have also discussed large-scale deployments of the home as a part of a hurricane-resistant community in Cameron Parish, Louisiana.

We had a five year reunion of the initiation of the project in February 2013. This allowed us to have a roundtable discussion with some of the primary players, and we conducted a public

RIGHT
BeauSoleil Five Year Roundtable

survey (some of the results are shown above.) We also had an open house with music from Caleb Elliot. It was a wonderful chance to reflect and celebrate our accomplishments.

And although an overwhelming majority of survey respondents (75%) thought that UL Lafayette should compete in another Solar Decathlon, there are currently no plans to do so. As stated in the introduction, this is probably a once in a lifetime experience. However, I have proposed a sort of regional Decathlon wherein a smaller group of universities, design/build and leave homes on a specific site for actual families to live in. Collaboration among teams and affordability would be paramount. The jury is still out on this idea. Stay tuned.

For now, the lone BeauSoleil Home stands on the edge of the UL Lafayette campus as a hopeful reminder of what sustainable housing might look like. It is adjacent to Girard Park so the public has easy access for viewing. Her cypress is graying, but other than that she is weathering well. So maybe she is no longer my baby. The BeauSoleil Home is a young adult who is now a highly-productive member of society.

The Descendants of the BeauSoleil Home

THE BEAUSOLEIL HOME HAS BEEN THE PROGENItor of several subsequent projects. The homes that follow in the footsteps of the BeauSoleil Home draw inspiration but do not slavishly copy BeauSoleil. In fact, the six homes built after BeauSoleil, explore other ends of the spectrum.

- The BeauSoleil Home is nomadic and now placed in a somewhat suburban setting - the new homes are very urban, located on lots less than 50 feet wide, near downtown.
- The BeauSoleil Home was prefabricated and modular - the new homes are site built with standardized components assembled in unique ways.
- The BeauSoleil Home was primarily built by students - the subsequent homes are an equal mix of student and contractor labor.
- The BeauSoleil Home had a generous budget ($375 per square foot or $188 per square foot for the production model) - the other homes have much smaller budgets ($72 to $115 per square foot.)
- The BeauSoleil Home was small (800 square feet) - the other homes are bigger (964 to 1,508 square feet). However, they are still much, much smaller than the regional average of 2,400 square feet.[121]
- The BeauSoleil Home represents a certain idealized form designed to appeal to all - the other homes are much more site-specific and client-specific.

The comparisons between the BeauSoleil home and all of the subsequent homes are continuing to provide valuable data. The appendix features a chart displaying quantitative comparisons and averages of the BeauSoleil Home and its descendants/cousins. With each new home we are able to raise the bar in terms of quality, sustainability, and affordability. This is BeauSoleil's ongoing legacy.

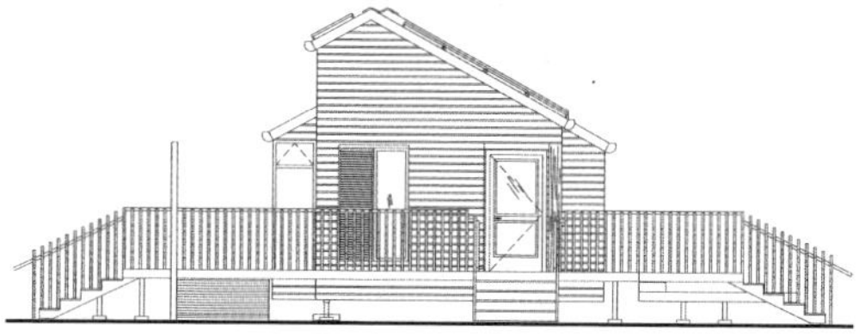

BEAUSOLEIL
LOUISIANA SOLAR HOME

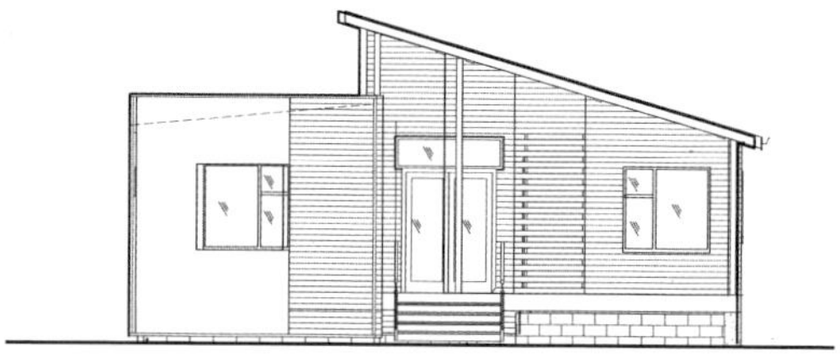

EVENThouse

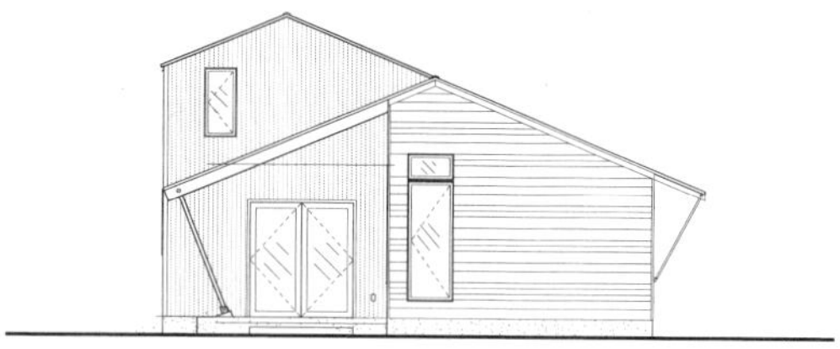

NEXThouse

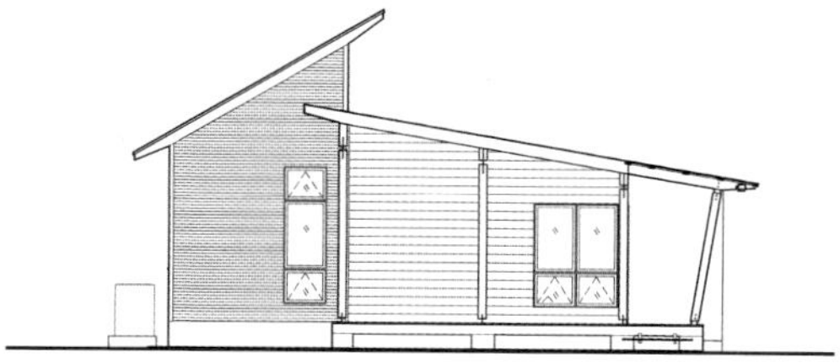

COURhouse

In 2010, the Lafayette Public Trust Financing Authority approached the School of Architecture and Design's Building Institute and proposed a partnership to build urban infill homes and sell them on the market to the public.[122] After a year of contract negotiations, the EVENThouse was designed by graduate architecture students and built with a local contractor in 2011. In the following two years, the NEXThouse and the COURhouse were built. The effects of these three urban homes are still being realized. But apparent immediately was a mood swing in the urban core neighborhoods around downtown Lafayette. These areas had not seen any new development in thirty to forty years. Although one home cannot change a neighborhood, maybe three or more can.

In addition, Lafayette Habitat for Humanity partnered with the School's Building Institute to design and build two homes in 2011 and 2013. And another is being built in 2014-2015. Like the Public Trust's Neighborhood Infill Program, the Habitat homes are being built in an urban core neighborhood as a part of a revitalization effort. And like the EVENT, NEXT, and COURhouses, the aim is to elevate sustainable design in affordable house models albeit with a much more modest budget.

Although it is the elder relative, I like to refer to the BeauSoleil Home as the country cousin of these other six homes. Every year when students begin designing the new home that will be built the following summer, they start by analyzing the BeauSoleil Home and its cousins. And then an interesting thing happens. Although I do not push them towards a particular aesthetic and they are not copying the previous designs, there seems to be a resemblance that develops. There is a familiarity. And this happens when you look at the homes on the street in their neighborhood. They are obviously different: they are newer, more contemporary, and use some different materials. But they also fit in. The proportions, roof angles, porches, and opening sizes begin a conversation with the older homes. Everyone who looks at the EVENThouse, NEXThouse, and COURhouse can recognize this. The homes are respectful of their surroundings but also assertive of their individuality. To use architectural historian Kenneth Frampton's term, they represent a sort of critical regionalism.[123] They are sympathetic to traditional forms, but critical of them and unabashedly modern.

The homes' simplicity and honesty of expression make them easy to accept. Like the BeauSoleil Home, if you squint your eye, you see the traditional house forms in the "cousins." And like the BeauSoleil Home, the EVENThouse, NEXThouse, and COURhouse are about the way people live. They were not designed to simply look good on the pages of *Dwell* magazine. First and foremost, they were designed to function and facilitate day-to-day life. And most importantly, they help the owners celebrate the rituals of life. Whether inviting people to watch a movie, dancing before a festival, or hosting a crawfish boil, the homes are gracious and accommodating.

Of interesting note, the homeowners of the three homes are quite diverse in their background and their reasons for purchasing the homes. Kirk Warner, who owns the EVENThouse, is in his 60s. He lived all over the country before coming back to Louisiana. Warner is a sheet metal/structural helicopter mechanic. He purchased the home because he appreciated the technology of the radiant heating/cooling plenum and he wanted to be near downtown.

Catherine Landers, who owns the NEXThouse, is a 20-something band director at Paul Breaux Middle School. The NEXThouse is her first house and it just made practical sense to have a small house near her work. And Elizabeth "EB" Brooks, the design director of Lafayette's Central Park ("the Horse Farm") bought the COURhouse somewhat impulsively at the open house the night it went on sale. She has an ecological and design/planning background which obviously added to her appreciation of the home's design and sustainability features.

TOP
EVENThouse

MIDDLE
NEXThouse

BOTTOM
COURhouse from NEXThouse

Landers says that she feels like she is part of "the progressive movement" that the BeauSoleil Home helped initiate. She says that there is "a stirring within Lafayette to come-together"[124] to make things better. The details and the functionality of the home, paired with its economical price

Homeowners

Kirk Warner, Catherine Landers, & Elizabeth Brooks

Thus far in the historical legacy of the BeauSoleil Home, there have been three BeauSoleil-like homes built and sold to local Lafayette residents. Built through a partnership between the city of Lafayette and the architecture department of UL Lafayette, the new homes are like the thriving offspring of the BeauSoleil Home, sharing many of the design elements and energy systems that were put in place by the students.

HOPE:
"Hope is the idea that life can be better."
–Warner

Born in Deridder and raised in Lake Charles, Louisiana, Kirk Warner is one of the first owners of the BeauSoleil Home's descendants. A self-described "Renaissance man," Warner purchased the EVENThouse in 2012. "I've always been open to things that are new and different," says Warner. "And I tend to look at things from a little different angle. I saw a rendering of the EVENThouse, and I liked it. I've always liked a simple, yet modern look to things. Then I read up on the house and learned it was green, energy-efficient, and low maintenance. That was all very appealing to me. The house is beautiful. Also, I live alone, so it's a great bachelor pad."

HOPE:
"I believe that the BeauSoleil project can help revitalize older neighborhoods and provide hope to people by providing affordable, reliable, and sustainable housing to families regardless of socioeconomic status."
–Landers

Catherine Landers is a teacher and band director at Paul Beaux Middle School. Her father, a successful entrepreneur, always advised her to make smart investments. She did just that by purchasing the NEXThouse, which is located in Lafayette's Freetown neighborhood. "I happened to be in the market for a house and I ended up taking a tour of the NEXThouse and fell in love with it," says Landers. "My favorite aspect of the house is the overall symmetry and the loft. I really like the idea of investing in something that I believe in. And the idea of a self-sustainable house seemed to be a good investment – lower bills through the use of solar energy and things like that. I think you should take risks on things you believe in."

COURhouse owner E.B. Brooks was born in Fayetteville, AR, and graduated from UL Lafayette with a degree in Renewable Resources. She is now Director of Planning & Design for Lafayette Central Park (formerly known as the Horse Farm). "I love the COURhouse and am a very satisfied homeowner for many reasons," says Brooks. "The layout, the natural light, the materiality, all work very well – both functionally and aesthetically. Having sustainable technologies all reduce my footprint significantly, and I feel that they offer a unique opportunity to showcase to other neighbors and passers-by what sustainable design can look like.

HOPE:
"Hope is the belief that your actions and attitude do make a difference in this world and that they inspire others to believe that they have that same power."
–Brooks

motivated her to buy it. According to Landers, the NEXThouse has the personal touches that a normal house wouldn't have. "The selling point are the shelves."[125] These were made lovingly by the students from salvaged/scrap material for the loft.

Landers is an optimist. Her friend says that she is "hopefully hopeful! Maybe that's why I bought the home."[126] Landers says that the NEXThouse has inspired her to live more sustainably. She did not grow up that way. In fact now her mother calls her a "hippie" for recycling! But she says "it almost seems hypocritical to live in a house like this (the NEXThouse) and not live sustainably."[127] The Freetown neighborhood where the NEXThouse and COURhouse is located is predominately African American. She feels that everyone is highly protective of her. Homes like the NEXThouse, which bring a new segment of the population to urban areas, help encourage diversity and community.

Warner says it was the style of the home that first attracted him to the EVENThouse. When he first visited the home, he famously said, "great house. Too bad it's here." He still says he has reservations about the LaPlace neighborhood.[128] "There are a lot of renters. There is a lot of drug-dealing."[129] So sometimes he does feel a bit like he is in a walled-compound, but he is friendly with many neighbors. Building community is a work in progress. But Warner was extremely proud when he had a stranger say, "thank you for investing in the neighborhood!" And he likes to quote Paul Simon saying, "The thought that life could be better is woven indelibly into our hearts and our brains."[130]

Brooks feels that she "manifested" the COURhouse into her life.[131] She says, "Ten years ago...I started drawing my dream home on a spare page in the back of my notebook...Those sketches, 3D massings, and air flow diagrams are almost identical to this house."[132] Brooks sums up the features of her home as only a designer and planner can: "It (the COURhouse) affords me the opportunity to

TOP
EVENThouse Interior

MIDDLE
NEXThouse Interior

BOTTOM
COURhouse Interior

engage in conversations with interested residents about distributed infrastructure, and the benefits on the environment, as well as on my pocket book, which is critical for those who are looking to learn more before they invest in incorporating these techniques and technologies into their own homes."[133]

The sustainability features, aesthetics, and spaces are glorious, but all the homeowners, including Brooks, appreciate their average monthly electricity bills of less than $65 (in 2013-2014).[134] Sustainability and HOPE have a pay-off!

The Building Institute will continue to tackle the problem of affordable and sustainable housing. What form that may take remains to be seen - maybe denser single family homes or even multifamily solutions? UL Lafayette is part of a North American Consortium studying design/build programs in terms of their impact on students and the community. This initiative, called the Design/Build Exchange or dbX, is part of a six-year Canadian Partnership grant.[135] This often missing reflective portion of analysis and best practices will allow the Building Institute to expand its capacity in the community and region - and continue generating hope.

TOP
COURhouse at Night

ABOVE
COURhouse Interior

ACKNOWLEDGMENTS

ACKNOWLEDGMENTS

Over 200 students and faculty from the University of Louisiana at Lafayette put their hearts and souls into the BeauSoleil Louisiana Solar Home. And over 2,000 partners supported the effort. I cannot name them all here in the acknowledgment section, however most are listed in the appendix. They are for whom this book is written.

I begin with the most important people in my life, my family. My wife Germaine, and my daughters Alex and Elise gave me the strength and inspiration to be the faculty adviser for the BeauSoleil Home project and to begin the task of writing *Generating Hope.* Germaine is my anchor. My daughters are wise beyond their years. They make me laugh and give me hope for the future every day. I dedicate this book to them.

My parents gave me the discipline and work-ethic to complete the writing. They cultivated my passion for architecture and taught me to appreciate great design. My independent and successful sisters, Jo and Jill, inspire me on a daily basis, and my brothers-in-law, Popie Billeaud, Moose Billeaud, Whitney Gonsoulin, and Andre Billeaud showed me how to build and provided support many times.

When I began the book, I approached our most loyal partners for support. They did not hesitate. Holly and Smith Architects were again the first to come to our aid. The key institutions of our community: UL Lafayette, the School of Architecture and Design, the UL Lafayette Foundation, Lafayette Utility Systems, Lafayette Economic Development Authority, Lafayette Parish Convention and Visitor's Commission, the American Institute of Architects (South Louisiana and State Chapters), LUBA Casualty Insurance Company, Teche Area Builder's Association, and the Louisiana Architectural Foundation immediately stood behind the book project as they had stood behind the making of the home. And Marianne and William Gjertson, Ken Ardoin, Geraldine Ramsay,

James A. Chance, Marc W. Judice, and Jeffrey LaBorde, individually took it upon themselves to support the effort.

My colleagues support and inspire me on a daily basis. Professor Emeritus Edward J. Cazayoux is the BeauSoleil Home's number one advocate and my mentor. Eddie's knowledge and wisdom about Louisiana culture and history guided the BeauSoleil Home on the path to success. His foreword to this book places the reader squarely within the context of Louisiana and the history of the School of Architecture and Design. Eddie – you lead, teach, and inspire by rolling up your sleeves and doing the work required. Thank you.

Professor Hector LaSala is my teaching inspiration and mentor. Professors Brian Powell, Bob Henry, Kari Smith, Dan Burkett, and Denise John more than filled out the TEAM BeauSoleil infield. Professors Michael McClure and Corey Saft provided necessary injections of criticism, support, and humor throughout the project and continue to do so. Directors Robert McKinney and Thomas Sammons provided confidence and guidance throughout the process, and Dean H. Gordon Brooks offered unconditional and enthusiastic support.

Pliny Fisk III is in many ways, one of the Godfathers of the Solar Decathlon. He is also one of the greatest architectural eco-pioneers of the sustainability movement. I am honored that Pliny set the international and historical stage for the book in his opening essay. No one could have done it better.

The BeauSoleil Home was first and foremost a teaching tool. As I always say when I am complimented on the home, "It is the student's project, and they are to be complimented." We had an amazing student TEAM. In particular, I could not have conceived of, recruited, or even hired a better set of TEAM officers. Gretchen LaCombe Vanicor, the Student Project Manager, held us all together. She carried the weight of the BeauSoleil World on her shoulders with strength and poise. Student Project Architect Scott Chappuis's calm leadership helped us weather the storms and envision the future of sustainability. As the Student Construction Manager, Jeremy Credeur's discipline and strength guided the building and fabrication, and his work ethic set a high bar. Catherine Guidry, our Student Public Relations Officer, was the charismatic and joyful face of the TEAM. Her enthusiasm was always infectious. Our Student Safety Officer, Chris Leger, was our accomplished voice of reason and high-craft. Denisse Castro Dufreche, the Student Instrumentation

Officer, brought passion, humor, and focus to the TEAM, as did her husband, Christopher Dufreche, another Student Project Architect. Our third Student Project Architect, Greg Jefferson, carried our flame of optimism. Student Engineering Officers, William Depa, David Carroll, Marsela Jakup-Wood, Christian DePrins, and Colin Gould were undaunted in the face of technical complexity while surrounded by architects! Architecture student Timothy Dumatrait began the project and returned when we needed an infusion of motivation towards the end. I could continue, but there are so many students that I cannot thank them all for their critical involvement, passion, and hope they brought to the BeauSoleil Louisiana Solar Home. I believe it changed their lives in a highly positive way like it did mine.

Many people were interviewed for this book. Yours are the stories of the BeauSoleil Louisiana Solar Home. Reliving the project through your memories is unbelievably moving and special. Your portraits are a powerful testament to the project's impact.

I would like to thank Dege Legg, my co-writer and editor, for pushing me to pull it all together and keeping things in perspective. And no one could have captured the color and passion of the TEAM in the biographical Portraits better than Dege. His wisdom, focus, and organization helped create the "roux" of this "gumbo."

Chelsea Ellison talked through the initial concepts of the book and accompanied me on many of the interviews (taking beautiful 35 mm black and white portraits). Her objective and sensitive voice were definitely signposts on this long journey. My colleague, ProfessorJean Edwards has always been my most critical and objective editor. Garrett Armentor and Trent Husser, my graduate assistants over the last two years, helped immensely with research for the technical sidebars and other assorted tasks. Philip Gould provided the majority of the vivid photos in the book. They bring back memories like nothing else can. My cousin Todd Mouton gave some of the best advice to me on the book and originally connected me to Megan Barra and Dege Legg. Michael Martin at the UL Press agreed to publish the book before the first word was written. Thank you for the confidence and faith in me and the project. UL Press's Mary Duhé and James Wilson provided other critical eyes when needed, too. Finally, what you are looking at is the graphic brilliance of Megan Barra. Megan, you're the woman!.

Although these two individuals were tangentially involved

in the project as advisers and volunteers, they became powerful, spiritual sages for me: Elemore Morgan Jr. and Eldred Griffin "Griff" Blakewood, IV. Sadly, both men have left this world, but their legacy remains in some respect in the BeauSoleil Home.

Writing a book is like building house – putting all the pieces together to create a place, a place of life and the stories of those who inhabit it. This book was written for the TEAM and its PARTNERS. However, the BeauSoleil Home, and the book by extension, are intended to serve ALL the people of Louisiana. A place I call HOME.

APPENDICES

TEAM BEAUSOLEIL (2007-2009)

W. Geoff Gjertson, AIA
Professor / Lead Faculty Adviser

H. Gordon Brooks, II, FAIA
College of the Arts, Dean

Mark E. Zappi, Ph.D., P.E.
College of Engineering, Dean

STUDENT OFFICERS
Gretchen LaCombe Vanicor, Project Manager
Jeremy Credeur, Construction Manager
Scott Chappuis, Student Project Architect
Greg Jefferson, Student Production Architect
Catherine Guidry, Public Relations Officer
Chris Leger, Health and Safety Officer
Chris Dufreche, Team Contact/Student Production Architect
Denisse Castro Dufreche, Instrumentation Officer
William Depa, Electrical Officer

FACULTY MEMBERS
Professor Emeritus Edward J. Cazayoux, FAIA, Architecture
Professor Robert McKinney, AIA, Past Director, Architecture
Professor Hector LaSala, Architecture
Professor Brian Powell, Interior Design
Professor Thomas Sammons, Architecture
Professor Jerry Malinowski, Industrial Design
Professor Jean Edwards, Interior Design
Professor Michael McClure, RA, Architecture
Professor Corey Saft, Architecture
Associate Professor Kari Smith, Architecture
Associate Professor Andy Loewy, Industrial Design
Assistant Professor Andrew Sammataro, Architecture & Interior Design
Assistant Professor Dan Burkett, Architecture
Assistant Professor Brooke Davis, Industrial Design
Assistant Professor Onezieme Mouton, Architecture
Assistant Professor Sharon Pate, Fashion
Assistant Professor Melissa Utt, Architecture
Dr. Belur Ashok-Kumar, EECE
Dr. Griff Blakewood, Renewable Resources
E. Raymond DesOrmeaux, P.E.
Dr. Gwen Fontenot, Marketing
Dr. Lucy Henke, Marketing
Dr. Robert Henry, EECE
Dr. J. Denise John, SoAD
Dr. G.H. Massiha, ITEC
Dr. Geoff Stewart, Marketing

UNIVERSITY ADVISORY COUNCIL

Dr. E. Joseph Savoie - President, UL Lafayette
Ken Ardoin - Vice President, University Advancement
Griff Blakewood - Ph.D., Department of Renewable Resources
H. Gordon Brooks II - Dean, College of the Arts, FAIA
Dave Comeaux - Director, Planned Giving, CFRE
Bill Crist - Director, Physical Plant, AIA
E. Raymond DesOrmeaux - P.E., F.ASCE; F.AIC
Julie Simon-Dronet - Past Director, Public Relations
Julie Falgout - Executive Director, Foundation
Dan Hare - Past Executive Director, Alumni
Dr. Joby John - Dean, College of Business Administration
Dr. Steve Landry - Past Vice President, Academic Affairs/Past Provost
Robert McKinney - Past Director, Architecture and Design, AIA, LEED AP
Charles Richard - Director, Cinematic Arts Workshop
Dr. Mark E. Zappi - Dean, College of Engineering, P.E

COMMUNITY ADVISORY COUNCIL

John Breaux - Former Senator
Professor Emeritus Edward J. Cazayoux, FAIA
John N. Chappuis
Michael Doucet - BeauSoleil avec Michael Doucet
Joey Durel, President - Lafayette City-Parish
Rob Guidry - Past President & CEO, Chamber of Commerce
Robert Guercio - Eco-Entrepreneur
Randy Haynie - Principal, Hayne & Associates
Hyatt Hood - ERA, Stirling Properties
Terry Huval - Director, LUS
Valerie Keller - Past CEO, Acadiana Outreach Center
Steven J. Oubre - Principal, Architect's Southwest, AIA
Trula Remson - Principal, Remson-Haley-Herpin Architects, AIA
John Stege - Past President, LASBH
Margaret H. Trahan - President/CEO, United Way of Acadiana

BEAUSOLEIL STUDENT TEAM 2008

SPRING

All School Charrette
2nd Yr.- 50 students
3rd Yr.- 30 students

Arch 402
Gretchen Vanicor
Scott Chappuis
Jeremy Credeur
Chris Leger
Chris Dufreche
Catherine Guidry
Denisse Castro Dufreche
Tim Dumatrait
Chaz Kemp
Jaron Young
Guy Brignac
Jean Paul Accomando

DSGN 480 - Dr. John
Shelly Arnaud
Amanda Gautreaux
Dominique Hebert
Zayne Mseis
Vasavi Veerina
Chris Dufreche
Ashley Braquet
Bryant Netter
Clifford Couvillon
Justin Pittman
Andrew Ruduolph
Anthony Stuhldreher

Arch 482
Gretchen Vanicor
Scott Chappuis
Michael Quinones

Interior Design 202
Shelly Arnaud
Dominique Hebert
Kathleen McCall
Caitlin Mcnany
Kevyn Parenton
Madeline Pellerin
Michelle Romero
Vasavi Veerina
Ellen Ware
Stephanie Wittmann
Paige Andrews
Sabrina Barnum
Courtney Dugas
Amanda Gautreaux
Jacqueline Hemphill
Lane McDonald
Zayne Mseis,
Nora Patterson
Emily Raley
Michelle Simoneaux

SUMMER

Arch 480
Nick Choate
Malcolm LeBlanc
Marshall Sellers
Nathan Menard
Stephanie Bordelon
Sarah Young
Lauren Marlbourough

Arch 597
Corey Newell
Bryan Marks
Jared Petitjean
Chris Angelle
Rachel Azar
Ellen Cooper
Lee Merckle
Jonathan Marcantel

FALL

Arch 501
Gretchen Vanicor
Scott Chappuis
Jeremy Credeur
Chris Leger
Chris Dufreche
Catherine Guidry
Denisse Castro Dufreche
Tim Dumatrait
Greg Jefferson
Steven Gremlin

DSGN 311
Desiree Riley
Akeem Martin

DSGN 597
Graydon Zanyk

Fashion Class
Meghann Harney
Jamie Taylor
English Guillory

Industrial Design
(2-3 Week Charrette)
Azeez Alli-Balogun
Winifred Blewster
Andre Broussard
Simon Broussard
Michael Buquet
Ronald Clark
Jacques Dugal
Timothy Joshua
Samantha Lehrmann
Billy McDonald
Danielle Scoccimaro
Keaton Smith
Ross Usie
Jake Warren
Joshua Williams
Garrett Mosing
Andrew Viguerie
Julie Nicholson

DSGN 480 - Dr. John
Michael George Bartlett
Joseph Carlson
Jeronimo Cordova
Justin Paul Cortez
Brad Michael Domingue
Andre P. Dupre
David Adamson Harrison
Addison Choate Himes
Eric Dodd Kimbrough
Alan D. Merkle
Jessalyn Pourcio Newton
Christopher S. pate
Cateline Marie Quinn
Michael Andrew Quinones
Desiree Doucet Riley
Shari Kristen Thompson
Tony Crawford Vaccarella
Trevor Lynn Waller
Jonathan Sinclair Williams
Sarah M. Young

Marketing Class - Dr. Stewart
(1/2 Semester Project)
Matthew Ian Bejeaux
Jamie Elizabeth Blue
Cristin Layne Buckles
Erin H. Butler
Victor Keith Tyree Carstarphen
Dominique Lashonda Clayton
Dwana Sharae Day
Kelly M. Debaillon
Jason H. Devries
Sarah MIchel Ducote
Michael David Quinn
Joseph D. Harden
Bradley E. Johnson
Levi Austin Kastner
Lauren Rachelle Kuhn
John Seth LaHaye
Lindsay B. Lamb
Andrea Beth Lejeune
Abdule James Levier
Evan Levitan
Joshua Ian Martin
Haley Nicole McGill
John E. Mommer
Vicky Pakdimounivong
Shannon D. Perry
Alex C. Prejean
Sebastian L. Prevot
Stephen J. Sarver
Charles Henry Schilling
Christopher M. Segura
Jimi Kae Simoneaux
Howard J. Sinitiere
Molly C. Stutes
Joany L. Sylvester
Vu Duy Tran
Andrew C. Wagley
Amy Joann Wickenheiser
Lacey L. Wyatt
Keaton Williams Yeates

BEAUSOLEIL STUDENT TEAM 2009

SPRING

Arch 502
Gretchen Vanicor
Jeremy Credeur
Chris Leger

Arch 598
Gretchen Vanicor
Scott Chappuis
Jeremy Credeur
Chris Leger
Chris Dufreche
Catherine Guidry
Denisse Castro Dufreche
Greg Jefferson
Bryan Marks
Jared Petitjean

Arch 402
Brad Domingue
Trevor Waller
Jessalyn Newton
Joseph Carlson
Justin Cortez
Monica Angelette
Robbie Kemp
Tony Vaccarella
Trevor Ducote

DSGN 480: LEED for BeauSoleil
Stephanie Bordelon
Laura Netterville
Shelby Begnaud
Ashley Bell
Christopher Pate
Joseph Carlson
Adam Pettus
Megan Durio
Austin Duhon
Jennifer Young

Arch 482
Kimberly Trautman
Torrie Smith
Carolina Sanchez
Kerry Frey
Megan Durio
Steven Comeaux
Elizabeth Roundtree
Alan Merkle

Industrial Design 3rd Year
Marcelle Courtois
Nathaniel Deverich
Valerie Draves
Jason Guillory
Laura Hanks
Hunter Hebert
Alan Merkle
Matt Perera
Justin Pittman
Torrie Smith
Kim Trautman
John Walker

Engineering
Thomas Bosch
Jude Fusilier
Colin Gould
Christian De Prins
Jason Habbit
Mike Huggins
Ashish Nepal
David Carroll
William Depa
Marsela Jakub-Wood
Daniel Barry

Music
Andrew Smith
David L Boudreaux
Ben Sellers

ADDITIONAL TEAM MEMBERS 2010 & 2011

SPRING 2010

Andrew Connorton
Sean Boubede
Erick Stutes
Jason Lantier
Jacob Petit
Taylor Alphonso
Manish Patel

FALL 2010

Laura Bullinger
Rachelle Trahan
Jessica Degate

SPRING 2011

Mechanical Engineering Senior Projects
Melissa Budden
Shannon Dupuis
Jacob Kelly
Mark Manning
J. Rachel Whitney

Electrical Engineering
Alvin Zerangue
Salem Alghubari
Ryan Duplechien
Rayan Mourcy
Eiyad Samrkandy
Paul Darby
Hunter Boudreaux
Abdullah AlShehri
Ruwantha Dewundara
Joshe Domfang
Jonas Thibodeaux

BEAUSOLEIL PARTNERS

GENERATING HOPE BOOK SPONSORS

Louisiana Contractor's Educational Trust Fund
LUBA Casualty Insurance Company
Lafayette Parish Convention & Visitors Commission
Lafayette Utility System
The Louisiana Architectural Foundation
Lafayette Economic Development Authority
Teche Area Builders Association
American Institute of Architects Louisiana
South Louisiana Chapter of American Institute of Architects
Geraldine Ramsey
Marianne & Bill Gjertson
Ken Ardoin
James A. Chance
UL Lafayette Foundation
Marc W. Judice
Jeffrey Laborde

HOME PARTNERS

CYPRESS TREE PARTNERS
($100,000 and over)

University of Louisiana at Lafayette
U.S. Department of Energy/ National Renewable Energy Lab
Lafayette Public Trust Financing Authority

LIVE OAK PARTNERS
($25,000 – $99,999)

American Power Association- DEED
Associate General Contractors- Louisiana Contractors Educational Trust Fund
Cinematic Arts Workshop- UL Lafayette
The Cypress Lumber Products Group
Lafayette Chamber of Commerce
Lafayette Conventions and Visitors Center
Lafayette Utility System
Louisiana Contractor's Educational Trust
Louisiana Department of Natural Resources
Louisiana System Built Homes
NanaWall
The Russo Group
Student Government Association- UL Lafayette
United Way of Acadiana

MAGNOLIA PARTNERS
($10,000 – $24,999)

Arlington Court Suites Hotel
Baltimore/Washington BeauSoleil Supporters
Bengal Transportation
BP America, Inc.
Breaux's Mart
Central Piers Inc.
Doug Ashy Building Materials
Ernest P. Breaux Electrical, Inc.
Gulf Coast Recovery Fund: Community Foundation of Acadiana
Jefferson Street Green Room
Lamar Advertising
Louisiana State Board of Architectural Examiners
Moulis Mechanical, Inc.
Renlita Doors North America, LLC
Sanyo
Teche Electric
Wells-Keown Lighting

CREPE MYRTLE PARTNERS
($5,000 – $9,999)

A/C Supply
American Community Renewable Energy Fund
American Institute of Architects - Louisiana
American Institute of Architects - South Louisiana
Associated General Contractors - Lafayette
Begneaud Manufacturing

Edmond Bentley
Billeaud Companies
Floyd P. Breaux Painting
John and Colleen Chappuis
Coburn Supply Company
Construction Specifications Institute - Lafayette
Professor Emeritus Edward J. Cazayoux
Roy T. Dufreche and Associates
Thomas E. Falgout, Sr.
Fox 15 KADN Lafayette
Andreé Gonsoulin
Philip Gould
Robert Guercio
Holly and Smith Architects
JB Mouton and Sons
Lafayette Steel Erector, Inc.
Landry House Movers
Louisiana Architectural Foundation
Louisiana Digital Reproduction
Louisiana Manufactured Home Association
LSE Crane Rental and Transportation
LUBA Workers' Comp
M & E Consulting
The Merlin Group, Ltd.
Metalhead
Mitsubishi HVAC and A/C Supply
Ron Murphy
Tom Norton
Fabian Patin
Southern Steel and Supply

PINE TREE PARTNERS
($1,000 – $4,999)

Abita Beer and Crescent Crown Distributing, Inc.
Addison and Associates
Tony Adrian
ADT Security Systems
Advanced Insulation Systems, LLC
Chad Aldridge
American Institute of Architects - New Orleans
ASHRAE
Lisa Ayres
Megan Barra
BeauSoleil Avec Michael Doucet
Martial F. Billeaud Sr. Foundation
Brand Scaffold Builders
Steve Breaux and Kathy Reed
C&C Technologies
Capital One
Cesco Chemicals
City Club at River Ranch
Coca-Cola Bottling Company
Cullen Investment Group, LTD
Frederic Daspit
Brooke Davis
Raymond DesOrmeaux / Randall Hebert
Wayne Domingue
Dupre Trucking
Dynamic Industries
Enphase Energy
Eunice Rental of Lafayette
Pliny Fisk III
Lynda Frese
Reese Fuller, rowgully.com
Gannett Foundation
John Geldersma
William and Marianne Gjertson
Global Data Systems
Doug and Diane Gonzales
Green Light Association & Pamplona
Theresa Guidry
Gerald and Martha Hebert
Grace and Hebert Architects, APAC

International Facility Management Assoc.-B.R.
Dutch Kepler
Kohler & The Plumbing Warehouse
Kraft, Gatz, Lane, Benjamin LLC
The LaCombe and Vanicor Families
Bryan Lafaye
Christine and Paul Lemaire
Dr. J. Lee Leonard, M.D.
Lighting and Electrical Associates, Inc.
Louisiana Solar Solutions
Lowry's Printing & Signs
MBCI
MED Express Ambulance Company
Clint Mouton
Oge's Rental
Steve Oubre, Architects Southwest
Party Rental Place
Paul & Lulu Hilliard Art Museum
Perlick
Jesse Poimboeuf
Port Building Specialties
Prevost Electric
Jim and Pat Prince
Quality Drywall, Inc.
Geraldine Ramsey
Realtor Association of Acadiana: Community Foundation of Acadiana
Rebirth Capital, LLC
Rotary Club of Lafayette
Marshal Sellers
Shreveland Constructors, LLC
Southern Pipe
Dennis Sullivan
United Tile of Lafayette
US Green Building Council - Louisiana Chapter
Ushio America, Inc.
Van Eaton and Romero
Way Down in Louisiana
Wooden Specialties, Inc.

ADOPT-A-STUDENT SPONSORS
(PINE TREE PARTNER, $1,000)

A & M Answering Services
Acadiana Mortgage Lenders Assn.
AIA Coastal Louisiana
Ken Ardoin
Barras Mueschke Architects
Edmond Bentley
Dean H. Gordon Brooks II
Green's Energy Group, LLC
E.G. "T-Boy" Hebert
Judice & Adley
Dr. Jeff LaBorde
Lemoine Company
M & E Consultants
Dr. Angela Mayeux-Hebert
Mary Morgan
Steve Oats
Geraldine Ramsay
Southern Cypress Mfg. Assn.
Teche Area Builders Assn.
Dean Charles W. Triche III
UL Lafayette Alumni Assn.

ROOM SPONSORS
(Refer partnership levels above)

Lafayette Public Trust Financing Authority - Transitional Porch
Lafayette Utilities System - Kitchen
UL Lafayette Student Government Association - Living Room
The Russo Group - Bathroom
Louisiana System Built Homes - Studio/Bedroom
Department of Natural Resources - Exterior Decking & Landscaping

FRIENDS
(Under $1,000)

John Anderson
Philip Billeaud
David Border
Bobby Butcher
James Chance
Richard Chappuis
David and Susan Comeaux
Taylor Davis
Blaise M. Dufrene, AIA
Richard G. Fullerton
Marc Judice
Emily and Sig Lanoux
Bryan and Therese LeBlanc
Rick LeBlanc
Robert McKinney
Julia D. Moroux
Gail Romero
Robert Smith
Chuck and Janet Wood
Doug and Tanya Yentzen
Louise and Bob Fryklund
Marcel Quimby
Melanie Francois
Bernard Fruge
John and Barbara Girard
William and Amy King
Dr. Mary B. Neiheisel
F. Wayne and Cheryl T. Stromeyer
Lawrence Baldwin and Laura Brown
William Morrison
Louis Banos
Carl J. Breaux, DDS
Daniel J. Carroll, M.D.
Chip Carter
Sydney Casselman
Wayne Domingue
Peter Hetzel
Gail and William Henry Hood
Red Lerille
W.M. and Betty Lowry
Karen E. Molloy
Donald Montie
John V. Raymond
Carol Ross
Dr. Conway G. Yarbrough
Marsela Jakup-Wood and Destari Djaphar
Dawn A. Humphrey
Carole G. Lancon
George T. Langlois
Phil and Bernadette Lank
Jeannie Prudhomme
Brooke Hamilton
Amy Elizabeth Alluma Lee
James Pecnik
Wendy Heflin
Jodie Manale
Warren and Mary Perrin
Janet A. Wilson
Linda M. Creamer
A La Carte
Antoni's Italian Café
Carraba's Italian Grill
Chris' Poboys
Dwyer's
Golfballs.com
Hub City
Iberia Bank
Iberia Parish Driving Range
Imonelli's
Kitchen Store
LaFondas
Lisa Karon Salon
Massage Envy
Olive Garden
Outback Steakhouse
Petes
Posados
Prejeans Restaurant
Riverspa
Schlotzsky's
Shangri-La
Texas Roadhouse
The Grande Theatre
The Great Escape Water Massage
Zeas
Lowe's
Steine's
Chastant's
Doug Young Nursery
Eco Nursery
The Liriope Factory
The Water Gardens Unlimited
Sunset Herbs
Southwest Safety Training
Louisiana Interchurch Conference
Water Gardens Unlimited
Lowry's Printing and Copying
Port City Tarp
Chef Bobby and Dot Catering
Chef Pat Mould
Pearson Cross
Coca-Cola Bottling Company
Crystal Cottage, Inc.
Event Rental, Inc.
Mrs. Stacey Boudreaux Grow
L'Eglise, Inc.
Louisiana Department of Transportation & Development
Marcello's Wine Market
Paradise Plantscapes, Inc.
Party Central
St. Patrick's Catholic Church
Terry Huval and The Jambalya Band
UL Lafayette Development Office
World of Wings
Annie D. Bourgeois
Melanie Francois
John and Barbara Girard
Diana Hinds
LeRoux
Charlotte Roberts
Douglass Winn
Edge Communications
KV Corporation
Petroquest Energy LLC.
St. Patrick's Church
Samantha Olivier
Kay and Albert Rees
Dennis Sulivan
Gaudin Equipment and Supply
W.m. and S.e. Guidry
Elite Fitness and Kettleball Systems
Electronic Payment Systems
Business First Bank
Lafayette Master Gardeners
J.D. Morein
Bosco Fabricators
LM Curbs
Allergy, Asthma, and Immunology Center of SW LA
Brook St. Partners, LLC
Famille Beausoleil Broussard
Fugro-Chance
LA Fish Fry
Deano Hardwoods

Louisiana Solar Solutions, Colin Bercier
Paul's Jewelry
Norbert and Patricia Langlinais
Gerami Flooring
Smith's Welding Service
Wattstopper
Gutter Company
Chappuis Property
Coleman Partners Architects, LLC
Friends of the Humanities- UL Lafayette
Shaw Environmental
Turner Industries
UL Ragin Cajun Football Team
Barbara Abdalla Black
Dr. Jay Culotta
Whitney Gonsoulin
Star Measurement Sales & Service, Inc.
Wright-Gilyard and Associates Real Estate
Charles B. Allen
Aline Arceneaux
Louis Banos
Mary Ann & Richard Britton
Rae and Bill Brodnax
Chip Carter
Sydney Casselman
Dennis & Sharon Gautreaux
Tracey Hanson
Peter Hetzel
Gail and Henry Hood
Fred Hoyt
Willanna E. Curley James
W.M. and Betty Lowry
Carolyn McClung
Karen E. Molloy
Donald Montie
Dr. Conway G. Yarbrough
Allen & Brenda Broussard
John & Toni Daigre
Dawn A. Humphrey
Dr. D.R. Jaubert
Carole G. Lancon
George T. Langlois 5
Phil and Bern Lank
Perret
Jeannie Prudhomme
Carinne O. Randazzo
Brooke & Susan Hamilton
Amy Elizabeth Allums Lee
James Pecnik
Lori Beaston
Patricia Cottonham
Marjorie B. Gardner
Garett P. Gauthier
Wendy Heflin
Sally M. Chappuis Kilchrist
Jodie Manale
Ramona B, McDaniel
Warren and Mary Perrin
Janet Wilson
Ruth & Stony Landry
Linda M. Creamer

COMMUNITY PARTNERS

Robert Bergeron
John Breaux - Former Senator
Professor Emeritus Edward J. Cazayoux
John N. Chappuis
Michael Doucet - BeauSoleil avec Michael Doucet
Joey Durel, President - Lafayette City-Parish
Andreé Gonsoulin
Philip Gould
Robert Guercio - Eco-Entrepreneur
Theresa Guidry - Lafayette Parish Master Gardener
Rob Guidry - President & CEO, Chamber of Commerce
Randy Haynie - Principal, Haynie & Associates
Randall Hebert
Hyatt Hood - ERA, Stirling Properties
Terry Huval - Director, LUS
Valerie Keller - Past CEO, Acadiana Outreach Center
Colleen McDaniel
Steven J. Oubre - Principal, Architects Southwest
Francis X. Pavy
Trula Remson - Principal, Remson-Haley-Herpin Architects
Tad Sabastian
Arla and John Slaughter
John Stege - President, LASBH
Mark Stielper
Keith Thibodeaux
Ken Thibodeaux
Margaret H. Trahan - President/CEO, United Way of Acadiana

UNIVERSITY PARTNERS

Dr. E. Joseph Savoie - President, UL Lafayette
Dr. Ray P. Authement - Past President, UL Lafayette
Dr. Steve P. Landry - Past Vice President, Academic Affairs/Past Provost
Ken Ardoin - Vice President, Advancement
Jerry Luke LeBlanc - Vice President, Administration and Finance
H. Gordon Brooks II - Dean, College of the Arts
Dr. Mark E. Zappi, P.E. - Dean, College of Engineering
Dr. Joby John - Dean, College of Business Administration
Robert McKinney - Past Director, Architecture and Design
Darleen Lugenbuhl - Past Development Director
John T. Landry - Past Development Director
Griff Blakewood, Ph.D. - Department of Renewable Resources
Dave Comeaux - Director, Planned Giving, CFRE
Bill Crist - Director, Facility Management
Julie Falgout - Executive Director, UL Lafayette Foundation
Dan Hare - Past Executive Director, UL Lafayette Alumni Association
Charles Richard - Director, Cinematic Arts Workshop
Kathleen Thames - Past Director, Communications and Marketing
Julie Simon-Dronet - Past Director, Public Relations
Dr. Robert Stewart - Past Vice President for Research
Ruth Landry, Director of Research
Father Chester Arceneaux
Valerye Boles
Dr. DeWayne Bowie
Rae Brodnax
Sue Broussard
Lark Chartier
Melanie Comeaux
E. Raymond DesOrmeaux
Jill Duhon
Jim Foret
Paulette Gilger
Gerald Hebert
Dr. Ramesh Kollura - Vice President for Research
Dr. Arun Lakhotia
Liz Landry
Sean Manuel
Martha Marse
Christine Payton
Joey Pons
Kathy Rosenberg
John Wales

COMPETITION RESULTS

SUBJECTIVE CONTEST SCORES (Judged by Juries of Experts)

	ARCHITECTURE	MARKET VIABILITY	ENGINEERING	LIGHTING DESIGN	COMMUNICATIONS
Max Points	100	100	100	75	75
UL Lafayette	78	97	79	64	53
Milwaukee	64	76	67	60	49
Missouri	64	87	72	65	61
Arizona	86	79	87	60	45
Rice	95	93	84	63	65
Alberta	80	81	77	65	62
Ontario/BC	91	89	79	69	67
Iowa State	61	92	88	63	66
Penn State	67	87	93	70	63
Spain	72	80	84	60	56
Kentucky	71	84	77	57	52
Ohio State	82	91	84	58	65
Boston	87	87	80	65	63
Germany	94	91	91	70	53
Virginia Tech	94	90	88	65	56
Cornell	70	89	81	65	67
Puerto Rico	74	85	85	66	42
Minnesota	81	91	96	72	59
California	98	92	95	68	70
Illinois	77	86	88	71	61

OBJECTIVE CONTEST SCORES (Metered/Instrumented - Except Entertainment Dinner)

	COMFORT ZONE	HOT WATER	APPLIANCES	HOME ENTERTAINMENT	NET METERING
Max Points	100	100	100	100	150
UL Lafayette	72	7	78	76	0
Milwaukee	63	45	62	64	0
Missouri	51	85	65	71	101
Arizona	49	73	70	65	0
Rice	67	85	51	48	100
Alberta	80	79	62	86	100
Ontario/BC	91	94	89	71	110
Iowa State	67	71	43	64	101
Penn State	60	64	54	71	0
Spain	54	33	64	66	109
Kentucky	65	78	70	75	105
Ohio State	82	62	51	60	101
Boston	58	79	53	53	44
Germany	92	95	89	87	150
Virginia Tech	72	57	43	47	101
Cornell	64	86	56	86	100
Puerto Rico	70	75	64	61	0
Minnesota	78	88	91	88	101
California	63	95	93	92	100
Illinois	92	100	94	93	137

UL LAFAYETTE SUMMARY

CONTESTS	RANK
Market viability	1
Appliances	6
Comfort zone	7
Home entertainment	7
Architecture	11
Lighting design	13
Engineering	15
Communications	16
Net metering	16
Hot water	20

FINAL 2009 SOLAR DECATHLON RANKING

1. Germany
2. Illinois
3. California
4. Ontario/BC
5. Minnesota
6. Alberta
7. Cornell
8. Rice
9. Kentucky
10. Ohio State
11. Missouri
12. Iowa State
13. Virginia Tech
14. Spain
15. Boston
16. Penn State
17. Puerto Rico
18. Arizona
19. UL Lafayette
20. Milwaukee

(Source: Solar Decathlon.org/Note: Scores have been rounded to nearest whole number and team names have been abbreviated.)

BEAUSOLEIL LOUISIANA SOLAR HOME AWARDS

(Refer to Bibliography for additional Information and publications)

LIFETIME ACHIEVEMENT.
InDesign: INNOV8 Award for BeauSoleil Home from *The Independent*. 2013.

POPULAR MECHANICS MAGAZINE.
BeauSoleil Home selected as one of 14 Best New Technologies for Greener Homes.
Awarded April 2010.

SOLAR DECATHLON 2009. Selective International Competition.
First Place Market Viability Contest.

SOLAR DECATHLON 2009 Selective International Competition.
First Place People's Choice Award.

DESCENDANTS HOME COMPARISON

BeauSoleil FAMILY TREE FRONT	DATE	DESIGN DURATION	CONSTRUCTION DURATION	SIZE	ACTUAL COST W/O LAND	COST PER SF	STUDENT VS. CONTRACTED LABOR OR OTHER VOLUNTEERS	SUSTAINABILITY STANDARD	NUMBER OF STUDENTS
	2007 to 2009	330 Days	330 Days	800sf (1,500 sf decks/ ramps)	$300 K ($150K for production model)	$375/sf	90% vs. 10%	L.E.E.D. Platinum	8 officers 200 other students
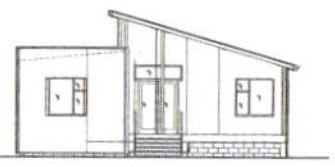 EVENThouse	2010 to 2012	250 Days	315 Days	1350 sf (580 sf porch)	$155 K	$115/sf	50% vs. 50%	National Green Building Standard Silver	3 officers 10 other students
 NEXThouse	2011 to 2012	240 Days	215 Days	1309 sf (418 sf porch)	$145 K	$111/sf	60% vs. 40%	National Green Building Standard Silver	7 officers 20 other students
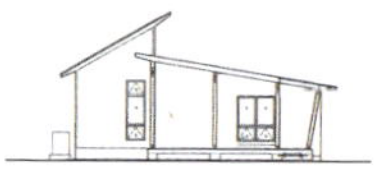 COURhouse	2012 to 2014	260 Days	290 Days	1508 sf (600 sf porch/ court)	$170 K	$113/sf	55% vs. 45%	L.E.E.D. Silver	6 officers 20 other students
 MS. LOUIDA'S	2010 to 2011	260 Days	150 Days	964 sf (280 sf porch/ patio)	$78 K	$81/sf	30% vs. 70%	Habitat for Humanity Standards	3 officers 8 other students
 MS. YOSHONNA'S	2012 to 2014	250 Days	180 Days	1264 sf (240 sf porch)	$100 K	$79/sf	10% vs. 90%	Habitat for Humanity Standards	3 officers 3 other students
 MS. WANDA'S	2013 to 2014	260 Days	120 Days (estimate)	1178 sf (590 sf porch)	$85 K (estimate)	$72/sf (estimate)	50% vs. 50% (estimate)	Habitat for Humanity Standards	6 officers 10 other students (estimate)
	7 YRS.	264 Days AVG. DESIGN DURATION	.198 Days AVG. CONSTRUCTION DURATION	1196 sf AVG. SIZE	$1.033 MILLION TOTAL	$95/sf w/o BS. AVG.	49% STUDENT LABOR AVG.	3 STANDARDS	307 STUDENTS TOTAL

NOTES

[1] *CollinsDictionary.com*, s.v. "beau = beautiful," and "soleil = sun," accessed June 25, 2014, http://www.collinsdictionary.com/.

[2] "About Solar Decathlon," U.S. Department of Energy, Last updated April 4, 2014, http://www.solardecathlon.gov/about.html.

[3] "2009 Final Results. People's Choice Award," U.S. Department of Energy, Last updated April 5, 2010, http://www.solardecathlon.gov/past/2009/final_results.html.

[4] "*Bon Cher Camarade*" in the series *Folk Festival USA*, National Public Radio, 1980. "Cajun" is a term used in South Louisiana for the people that originally lived in Nova Scotia, Canada, in 1603. Though they had been under the rule of France, by 1713 they came under the rule of the British, and rather than swear allegiance to the British crown, they chose to maintain their independence in Nova Scotia. As a result of being French Catholic within what was then a British colony, the Cajuns, or Acadians as they were called then, came into conflict with the British.

[5] "*Bon Cher Camarade*" in the series *Folk Festival USA*, National Public Radio, 1980. "Creole" in South Louisiana originally referred to the large French and Spanish planters, people of Old World descent born in the New World. These Creoles brought slaves, mainly through the French West Indies and from what later became French West Africa. Through intermingling with these slave populations, a new middle population emerged that was neither fully African nor fully European. It was an Afro-French population. And this middle population, sometimes referred to as the "Creoles of color" or "black Creoles" are the basis for what we now call Creole society.

[6] At the time of this writing it is unlikely that the author will ever participate in future Solar Decathlons although this is always a possibility for another faculty member/entity of UL Lafayette.

[7] Although the author has been contemplating writing a book since the Decathlon occurred, it was not until December of 2012 that a decision was made and a deadline established.

[8] As stated in the Acknowledgments, writing a book is a lot like building a home: carefully and thoughtfully putting together a multitude of pieces to create something greater than its constituent parts. And in doing so, creating Place.

[9] Dege Lege, "This book should be like a victory lap." Mentioned in conversations to author in April 2014.

[10] According to the 2010 Census the median income for a household in Louisiana is $35,996.

[11] "Market Viability," U.S. Department of Energy, Last updated March 23, 2010, http://www.solardecathlon.gov/past/2009/contest_market_viability.html.

[12] The origin of the word "hope" is unclear. It may possibly be Germanic from the word "hop" meaning "leaping in expectation." (http://www.etymonline.com/index.php?term=hope.) The word is fascinating. Although it has its religious and spiritual connotations, it has become commonplace for everyday wishes and desires, too. In the biblical use of hope there is a connotation of certainty unlike the modern day definition of a wish or expectation. (http://bible.org/article/hope) And unlike most words, "hope" can be both noun and verb:

Noun

1. the feeling that what is wanted can be had or that events will turn out for the best: *to give up hope.*
2. a particular instance of this feeling: *the hope of winning.*
3. grounds for this feeling in a particular instance: *There is little or no hope of his recovery.*
4. a person or thing in which expectations are centered: *The medicine was her last hope.*
5. something that is hoped for: *Her forgiveness is my constant hope.*

Verb

6. to look forward to with desire and reasonable confidence.
7. to believe, desire, or trust: *I hope that my work will be satisfactory.*

(http://dictionary.reference.com/browse/hope)

[13] Refer to the Glossary of Architectural Terms in the Appendices for specific definitions.

[14] *CollinsDictionary.com*, s.v. "joie = joy," "de = of," and "vivre = life," accessed June 25, 2014, http://www.collinsdictionary.com/.

[15] Al Gore, *An Inconvenient Truth* (New York: Rodale, 2006), 306.

[16] Edward J. Cazayoux,. interview by W. Geoff Gjertson, Breaux Bridge, La., June 21, 2013.

[17] "2007 Teachers Seminar," Association of Collegiate Schools of Architecture, https://www.acsa-arch.org/programs-events/conferences/teachers-seminar/2007-teachers-seminar.

[18] W. Geoff Gjertson, "Mission Statement," Building Institute, University of Louisiana at Lafayette, Last updated April 3, 2006, http://buildinginstitute.louisiana.edu/about-us/mission-statement.shtml.

[19] "Maison de Culture," Vermilionville Living History and Folk Life Park, Lafayette, Louisiana. http://bayouvermiliondistrict.onlinemarketingconsole.com/vermilionville-spotlights/historic-homes.

[20] Hector LaSala, "The Building Institute: A Civic-Engagement Instrument," *New York Times*, August 9, 2006, http://www.nytimes.com/2006/08/09/college/collegespecial2/coll-adp-building.html?pagewanted=print&action=click&module=Search&region=searchResults&mabReward=relbias%3Ar&url=http%3A%2F%2Fquery.nytimes.com%2Fsearch%2Fsitesearch%2F%23%2Fhector%2Blasala%2Bbuilding%2Binstitute%2F&_r=0.

[21] Julia Mandell, "Up to Speed," *Metropolis Online Magazine*, May 2006, http://www.metropolismag.com/May-2006/Up-to-Speed/building.html?ex=1160884800&en=0114d2709a0613f3&ei=5070&_r=0.

[22] "Montessori education is an educational approach developed by Italian physician and educator Maria Montessori and characterized by an emphasis on independence, freedom within limits, and respect for a child's natural psychological, physical, and social development." "Montessori education," Wikipedia, Accessed 2014, http://en.wikipedia.org/wiki/Montessori_education.

[23] "(The Bauhaus) was founded with the idea of creating a "total" work of art in which all arts, including architecture, would eventually be brought together." "Bauhaus," Wikipedia, Accessed 2014, http://en.wikipedia.org/wiki/Bauhaus.
[24] "2007 Southeast Fall Conference," Association of Collegiate Schools of Architecture,
http://acsa-arch.org/programs-events/conferences/fall-conference/2007-southeast-fall-conference.
[25] "2007 Solar Decathlon: Texas A&M," U.S. Department of Energy, Last updated February 18, 2010, http://www.solardecathlon.gov/past/2007/team_texasam.html.
[26] "Biography," Shigeru Ban, 2014 Laureate, The Pritzker Architecture Prize, The Hyatt Foundation, 2014.
http://www.pritzkerprize.com/laureates/2014.
[27] Carolyn Kormann, "Shigeru Ban: Shelter From The Storm," *The New Yorker*, October 2, 2011,
http://www.newyorker.com/online/blogs/festiva/2011/10/shigeru-ban-shelter-from-the-storm.html. From discussions with Shigeru Ban, the slogan "I hate waste," was printed on conference t-shirts.
[28] *Wikipedia.org*, s.v. "Hurricane Katrina," Wikipedia accessed May 25, 2014, http://en.wikipedia.org/wiki/Hurricane_Katrina.
[29] Samuel Mockbee, quoted in "About Samuel "Sambo" Mockbee," 2009-2014, http://samuelmockbee.net/biography/.
[30] "Waterfront Development: Delcambre, Louisiana," Community Design Workshop, UL Lafayette, Delcambre Master Plan, PDF found on Louisiana Sea Grant website: www.laseagrant.org, Last updated on May 12, 2014,
http:// www.laseagrant.org/pdfs/delcambre_ulldesignworkshop.pdf.
[31] From the author's memory, it was Professor Michael McClure who first coined the term, "Solar D" and would later suggest "BeauSoleil," as the home's name.
[32] Malcolm Gladwell, *Outliers: The Story of Success* (New York: Brown and Company, 2008).
[33] David Epstein, *The Sports Gene: Inside The Science of Extraordinary Athletic Performance* (New York: Penuin Group, 2013), as quoted on CBS Sunday Morning, April 6, 2014. http://www.cbsnews.com/news/are-elite-athletes-born-or-made/
[34] Reference to William Shakespeare's, Julius Caesar and the book *Fault in our Stars* by John Green.
[35] "Solar Decathlon Frequently Asked Questions: How many teams apply?," U.S. Department of Energy, Last updated April 8, 2014, http://www.solardecathlon.gov/faqs.html. Although solardecathlon.org says that the number of applicants is confidential, we received an off-the-record amount of 40-50 from one of the organizers.
[36] W. Geoff Gjertson, "Louisiana Solar House: A Marketable Application," (Unpublished original position statement October 23, 2007).
[37] Two UL Lafayette Presidents supported the BeauSoleil Home: Dr. Ray Authement and Dr. Joseph Savoie. Under Dr. Savoie's administration, Liz Landry was instrumental in guiding the TEAM through procedures and approvals. The author is indebted to her frankness and support. Dr. Steve Landry, the University VP and Provost, also offered support and guidance.
[38] *Google.com*, s.v. "Facilitate," accessed May 25, 2014,
http://www.google.com/search?client=safari&rls=en&q=facilitate&ie=UTF-8&oe=UTF-8.
[39] W. Geoff Gjertson, Principle Investigator and Editor, *Solar Decathlon Proposal 2009* (Lafayette, La.: Self-Published, 2007), 1.
[40] The TEAM was anxious to find out if their proposal was accepted and had emailed NREL to find out the status. On January 11, 2009, the author received a phone call from NREL's Jeff Soltesz. UL Lafayette was the first team notified.
[41] W. Geoff Gjertson, email to UL Lafayette faculty, November 4, 2007.
[42] Hector LaSala, email to Onezieme Mouton and other UL Lafayette faculty, November 4, 2007.
[43] Michael McClure, email to UL Lafayette faculty, November 4, 2007.
[44] Michael Doucet, email to Hector LaSala, November 11, 2007.
[45] Carl A. Brasseaux, *The Road to Louisiana: The Saint Domingue Refugees in Louisiana,* ed. Glenn R. Conrad, (Lafayette, La.: Center for Louisiana Studies, University of Southwestern Louisiana, 1992).
[46] Architectural graphics are usually serious, dry, and monochromatic, to name a few common attributes.
[47] Hector LaSala, conversation with the author, 2013.
[48] "The Wizard of Cool," *Baton Rouge Sunday Advocate Magazine*, May 23, 1982.
[49] W. Geoff Gjertson, ed., "BeauSoleil Louisiana Solar Home Project Manual," (Lafayette, La.: Self-Published, June 2, 2009), 353-56. Also available online: http://www.solardecathlon.gov/past/2009/team_louisiana.html.
[50] "Lifestyles-ESRI Tapestry Segmentation," Environmental Systems Research Institute, www.ESRI.com/Tapestry. ESRI's Community Tapestry segments U.S. consumers into groups based on Life modes, Urbanization Levels, and Income Ranges. Two Tapestry market segment groups are "Prosperous Empty Nesters," and "Silver and Gold."
[51] Stuart Elliot, "The Older Audience is Looking Better Than Ever," *New York Times*, April 20, 2009, national edition, http://www.nytimes.com/2009/04/20/business/20adcol.html.
[52] "Studio 804 Mission," University of Kansas, Architecture, Design and Planning, http://studio804.com/.
[53] The questions were included as a part of the syllabus prepared for ARCH 402 by the author and Kari Smith.
[54] Irina Vinnitskaya, "The Zachary House / Stephen Atkinson Architecture," *ArchDaily*, October 20, 2012, Accessed May 25, 2014, http://www.archdaily.com/?p=282552> http://www.archdaily.com/282552/the-zachary-house-stephen-atkinson-architecture/.
[55] In interviews conducted with TEAM members Scott Chappuis, Gretchen LaCombe Vanicor, Chris Leger, and Tim Dumatrait, on June 10, 2013, and July 13, 2009, they consistently cited the Transitional Porch as their favorite part/element of the BeauSoleil Home.
[56] John Laudun, interview by W. Geoff Gjertson, Lafayette, La., July 10, 2013.
[57] M&E Consulting's Shane Hernandez, Jay Breaux, and Scotty Baudoin were instrumental in getting the BeauSoleil Home successfully designed. They gave it their all. The TEAM is indebted to them.

[58] W. Geoff Gjertson, ed., "BeauSoleil Louisiana Solar Home Project Manual," (Lafayette, La.: Self-Published, June 2, 2009), 350-51. Also available online: http://www.solardecathlon.gov/past/2009/team_louisiana.html.

[59] Ibid., 351.

[60] The TEAM is indebted to May Hays, who was with Teche Electric, for her continual support and enthusiasm.

[61] Ibid., 359-61.

[62] Ibid., 351-52.

[63] Author's estimate based on approximately 10 months of design, 10 months of building, 1 month of the competition, and 4 months of outreach/fundraising.

[64] "Mission," University of Louisiana at Lafayette, 2014, Accessed May 25, 2014, http://www.louisiana.edu/about-us/who-we-are/mission-vision-values.

[65] Dr. Arun Lakhotia, Director of the Cajunbot Program at UL Lafayette, had incredible success and was an inspiration and sounding-board for the author and TEAM.

[66]Although the Solar Decathlon did not publish the costs of the houses until the 2009 competition (http://www.solardecathlon.gov/past/2009/construction_costs.html), anecdotal evidence suggested the range of $500,000 to $2 million for each of the projects (not just the cost of the home but transportation, travel, etc.)

[67] Dr. Denise John's husband, Dr. Joby John, Dean of the College of Business was a great ally in the BeauSoleil Home project. The TEAM is indebted to him, his faculty, and the entire College of Business.

[68] Refer to Technical Sidebars.

[69] Catherine Guidry, email to TEAM and to NREL, June 10, 2009.

[70] "BeauSoleil Louisiana Solar Home Media Outreach Report," NHD.

[71] Conni Castille, first draft of script emailed to Author, August 14, 2008.

[72] "Communication Success: UL Lafayette TEAM BeauSoleil 2009," Dr. Denise John, W. Geoff Gjertson, Catherine Guidry, and Gretchen LaCombe Vanicor (Lafayette, La.: Self-Published, December 8, 2009), 5.

[73] Ibid., 6.

[74] Refer to the Appendix for a list of partners/sponsors.

[75] "Welcome Home. Bienvenue a la maison: Believe in tomorrow, Beginning today," ed. the Russo Group, Last updated 2011, http://www.beausoleilhome.org/content/home/index_2.html.

[76] "BeauSoleil Louisiana Solar Home Media Outreach Report," NHD.

[77] Denisse Castro, Scott Chappuis, Jeremy Credeur, Chris Dufreche, Catherine Guidry, Greg Jefferson, Chris Leger, and Gretchen LaCombe Vanicor, "BeauSoleil Louisiana Solar Home: Student Thesis Document," (Lafayette, La.: Self-Published, 2010), 35.

[78] Ben R. Rich and Leo Janos, *Skunk Works* (Sphere, 1995).

[79] Dave Taylor with Global Data Systems, Lafayette, La., loaned the warehouse webcam and set it up for TEAM BeauSoleil.

[80] Brian Powell, interview by W. Geoff Gjertson, Breaux Bridge, La., June 21, 2013.

[81] Edward J. Cazayoux, interview by W. Geoff Gjertson, Breaux Bridge, La., June 21, 2013.

[82] "Leadership in Energy & Environmental Design (LEED)," U.S. Green Building Council, Last modified 2014, http://www.usgbc.org/leed?gclid=COa82_Twx74CFeJF7AodQw4AoA.

[83] "About," URBANbuild, Tulane University, 2013, http://www.tulaneurbanbuild.com/index2.php#/rtext_2/1/.

[84] Dr. Mark Zappi, Dean of the College of Engineering, offered continual support and guidance. The TEAM is grateful for his efforts.

[85] Scott Chappuis, Email to TEAM, February 16, 2009.

[86] David M. Cheney, "USA Statistics by Province by Percentage Catholic," 1996-2005, http://www.catholic-hierarchy.org/country/spcus3.html.

[87] Sarah Spell, "Power House," *La Louisiane*, Spring 2009, 21.

[88] W. Geoff Gjertson, email to TEAM, June 1, 2009.

[89] Ernest P. Breaux Electric and Moulis Plumbing went above and beyond the call of duty for TEAM BeauSoleil. The author is indebted to them for their expertise, patience and understanding.

[90] "Plywood," Design Museum, http://designmuseum.org/design/plywood.

[91] Austin Williams, "Rainscreen cladding: letting air in to keep rain out," NBS Shortcuts, http://www.thenbs.com/topics/DesignSpecification/articles/rainscreenCladding.asp.

[92] "BeauSoleil," Elder Forest Products, d/b/a James Donald Elder, Cypress Lumber Specialist, http://www.eldercypresslumber.com/Beau.htm.

[93] In discussions with the author, Dan Rockhill described how he would make the students remove all the siding on the homes if it was not straight and reinstall it plumb and level.

[94] John K. Thibodeaux, interview by W. Geoff Gjertson, Breaux Bridge, La., May 17, 2013.

[95] Gretchen LaCombe Vanicor, email to Author, September 9, 2009.

[96] "About Solar Decathlon," U.S. Department of Energy, Last updated April 4, 2014. http://www.solardecathlon.gov/about.html.

[97] Ibid.

[98] Saquib Rahim, "The Quest to Build an "Ethically Responsible House," *New York Times*, October 9, 2009, Last updated 2009, http://www.nytimes.com/cwire/2009/10/09/09climatewire-the-quest-to-build-an-ethically-responsible-12926.html?pagewanted=all.

[99] "Solar Decathlon 2009: Contests and Scoring," U.S. Department of Energy, Last updated March 23, 2009, http://www.solardecathlon.gov/past/2009/contests_scoring.html.

[100] "Weather History for Washington DC," Weather Underground, http://www.wunderground.com/history/airport/KDCA/2009/10/1/MonthlyHistory.html.

[101] Theodorus of Samos, a Greek sculptor and architect, is credited with inventing the water level in the 6th century B.C.

[102] Landscape architect Roy Dufreche designed and selected the landscaping based on these Louisiana biomes: Bog, Coastal Plain, and Upland Hardwood. In addition, there was a productive vegetable garden.

[103] Arlington Court Suites Hotel, 1200 N. Courthouse Rd., Arlington, Va.

[104] Saquib Rahim, "The Quest to Build an 'Ethically Responsible House,' *New York Times,* October 9, 2009, Last updated 2009, http://www.nytimes.com/cwire/2009/10/09/09climatewire-the-quest-to-build-an-ethically-responsible-12926.html?pagewanted=all.

[105] Gretchen LaCombe Vanicor, "We Passed! We Passed! We Passed!," *TEAM BeauSoleil* Blog, October 8, 2009, http://believeinbeausoleil.blogspot.com/2009/10/we-passed-we-passed-we-passed.html.

[106] W. Geoff Gjertson, "Our Bedroom View," *TEAM BeauSoleil* Blog, October 9, 2009, http://believeinbeausoleil.blogspot.com/.

[107] "TEAM BEAUSOLEIL IS TOPS IN MARKET VIABILITY CONTEST," *TEAM BeauSoleil* Blog, October 12, 2009, http://believeinbeausoleil.blogspot.com/.

[108] TEAM BeauSoleil Still Celebrating Win," *TEAM BeauSoleil* Blog, October 12, 2009, http://believeinbeausoleil.blogspot.com/.

[109] Three of the homes that ended up consuming more electricity than they produced were on the end of the electrical grid, and TEAM BeauSoleil noticed that their inverter was tripped (turned-off several times). TEAM BeauSoleil's low energy production may not have been completely its fault.

[110] TEAM Officers Chris Leger and Jeremy Credeur were in charge of cooking the meals.

[111] Tom Norton, email to TEAM, October 8, 2009.

[112] It is interesting to note that in Timothy Lentz's 2010 Iowa State University thesis paper analyzing the passive features of the 2009 Solar Decathlon Homes, UL Lafayette had the second best daylighting (.17 effective aperature value) and the third best window/floor space ration (5.2%).

[113] Bengal Transport and their two truck drivers showed great dedication and patience. The TEAM is indebted to them.

[114] Wesley Pulkka, "Antoine Predock: architecture and time," *Trendmagazineglobal.com,* Fall 2009/Winter 2010, 63, *TEAM BeauSoleil* Blog, October 12, 2009, http://believeinbeausoleil.blogspot.com/.

[115] Ed Mazria, email to Eddie Cazayoux, October 30, 2009.

[116] Ozzie Zehner, *Green Illusions: The Dirty Secrets of Clean Energy and the Future of Environmentalism* (Lincoln: University of Nebraska Press, 2012).

[117] Megan Durio, in BeauSoleil Home Guest log book, March 14, 2010.

[118] Phylis Bonhager, in BeauSoleil Home Guest log book, March 27, 2010.

[119] BeauSoleil Reunion Google Survey April 30, 2013, https://docs.google.com/forms/d/1oNAZ7wIFx8Grv1WG-t9Fnrr_e_tUf2zyclwfbLVJfKk/viewanalytics.

[120] Ibid.

[121] The U.S. Census Bureau illustrates the irrational and inversely proportional growth of average American homes from 1950 (approximately 1,000 SF) to 2010 (approximately 2,400 SF) while at the same time average family sizes have decreased from 3.7 to 2.5.

[122] John Arceneaux of the LPTFA, has been a supporter of good sustainable architecture for years in Lafayette, LA. He had this vision to continue building homes. The author is indebted to him for his initiative.

[123] Kenneth Frampton, *Towards a Critical Regionalism: Six Points for an Architecture of Resistance*, In H. Foster, ed. *Postmodern Culture.* (London: Pluto Press, 1983).

[124] Catherine Landers, interview by W. Geoff Gjertson, Lafayette, La., June 14, 2013.

[125] Ibid.

[126] Ibid.

[127] Ibid.

[128] Kirk Warner, interview by W. Geoff Gjertson, Lafayette, La., June 14, 2013.

[129] Ibid.

[130] Ibid. Paul Simon song: http://thinkexist.com/quotation/the-thought-that-life-could-be-better-is-woven/364399.html.

[131] Elizabeth Brooks, email to Dege Legg, April 1, 2014.

[132] Ibid.

[133] Ibid.

[134] Catherine Landers and Kirk Warner, interview by W. Geoff Gjertson, Lafayette, La., June 14, 2013.

[135] "The dbX: What is it?," ed. Christopher Trumble, Last updated April 14, 2014, http://www.db-x.org/.

GLOSSARY OF ARCHITECTURAL TERMS

(Oxford Dictionary & Author's Definitions)

Active systems - Systems in buildings requiring energy or specialized equipment (i.e., Solar photovoltaics, mini-split heat pumps, or solar flat plate thermal collectors – if they have electric pumps).

Aesthetic - Aesthetics is a branch of philosophy dealing with the creation and appreciation of beauty. It is sometimes called a judgment of sentiment and taste.

Alternative Energy - Energy generated in ways that do not deplete natural resources or harm the environment, especially by avoiding the use of fossil fuels and nuclear power.

Aperture - Openings like windows and doors in buildings. Also called fenestration.

Awnings - Material stretched or mounted on a frame and used to keep the sun or rain off a storefront, window, doorway, or deck.

Battery-back-up - An uninterruptible power supply with a storage battery that provides emergency power to a load when the input power source fails or is unavailable.

Bifold door - A door capable of being folded into two parts that are hinged together.

Biomes - A large naturally occurring community of flora and fauna occupying a major habitat.

BIPV's - Building-integrated photovoltaics are solar cells that are integrated into roofing, exterior wall surfaces, or windows. See also PVs and Photovoltaics.

Blocking - Pieces of wood or other materials that provide support and attachment within a wall or other construction for mounted hardware such as cabinets, shelving, or other items.

Bousillage - A mixture of clay and Spanish moss or other fibrous substances used as the infill between the timbers of a half-timbered building, often in 18th-19th century Louisiana homes. See also Colombage.

Branding - The marketing practice of creating a name, symbol, or design that identifies and differentiates a product from other products.

Bump-out - An extension of a room or building that creates a projection in a wall.

CADD - Acronym for computer-aided design and drafting.

Carbon-neutral - Making no net release of carbon dioxide to the atmosphere.

CFL - A compact fluorescent lamp, also called compact fluorescent light.

Charrette - A meeting in which all stakeholders in a project attempt to brainstorm ideas, resolve conflicts, and map solutions.

Cistern - A tank for storing water, especially rainwater.

Cladding - The application of one material over another to provide a skin or layer intended to control the infiltration of weather elements, and for aesthetics. See also Rain-screen.

Clerestory - A high portion of an interior wall, sometimes rising above adjacent rooftops, and having windows admitting daylight to the interior.

CMU - Concrete Masonry Unit, generally used to construct masonry walls or raised foundation walls or piers.

Colombage - Timber construction using half timbers, that is, members measuring not less than 5" x 10" in cross section. Often infilled with bousillage in Louisiana.

Condenser - An apparatus or container for condensing vapor – usually refrigerant for – air-conditioning systems. Usually located outside the building envelope due to heat generated.

Constructability - A project management technique to review construction processes from start to finish during pre-construction phase. It identifies obstacles before a project is actually built to reduce or prevent errors, delays, and cost overruns. See also Solar Decathlon Market Viability Contest criteria.

Contextual - Architecture that responds to its surroundings by respecting what is already there.

Critical Regionalism - An approach to architecture that strives to counter the placelessness and lack of identity of the International Style (architecture), but also rejects the whimsical individualism and ornamentation of Postmodern architecture. (Term coined by Kenneth Frampton in 1983.)

Daylighting - The practice of placing windows or other openings and reflective surfaces so that during the day natural light provides effective internal lighting.

Deconstructivism - An architectural movement or style influenced by deconstruction that encourages radical freedom of form and the open manifestation of complexity in a building rather than strict attention to functional concerns and conventional design elements (such as right angles or grids).

DoE - The Department of Energy is a cabinet-level department of the United States government concerned with the United States's policies regarding energy.

Dogtrot - Historically consisted of two log cabins connected by a breezeway or "Dogtrot," all under a common roof. Typically one cabin was used for cooking and dining while the other was used as a private living space, such as a bedroom.

EPS - Expanded polystyrene is a lightweight cellular material consisting of fine spherical shaped particles that are comprised of 98% air and 2% polystyrene. This area is trapped within a number of closed hollow cells in each particle. Usually used for insulation.

Flat Plate Collector - A heat collector consisting of a series of flat glass or plastic plates with black metal surfaces that absorb solar energy for heating water or air.

Footprint - The entire area of ground covered by a permitable structure; in other words almost everything except pavement. Attached porches are still part of the footprint. Also refers to the amount of an individual person or home's energy/resource consumption. In the case of the Solar Decathlon, the area under the eaves, overhangs, or awnings was considered part of the footprint.

French-Style Windows - A French window is a large, door-sized, predominantly glass aperture, typically set in pairs or multiples thereof.

Furring-strips - A length of wood running perpendicular to roofing, siding, or flooring, designed to level or create a space behind the materials. See also rain-screen.

Galvalume - Trade name for a metal alloy coating that is composed of aluminum, zinc, and silicone. Similar to galvanized metal.

GFCI - Ground fault circuit interrupter, an electrical wiring device that disconnects a circuit whenever it detects that the electric current is not balanced between the energized conductor and the return neutral conductor.

Greywater - The relatively clean waste water from baths, sinks, washing machines, and other kitchen appliances.

Grid / Grid-tied - A network of synchronized power providers and consumers that are connected by transmission and distribution lines and operated by one or more control centers. When used by photovoltaic users, the grid provides a location to outsource excess electricity and is a source for power when the sun is not out. See also Net-metering.

Gutters and Downspouts - a shallow trough fixed beneath the edge of a roof for carrying off rainwater to a pipe or downspout to the ground or to a cistern for collection.

Halogen - An incandescent lamp that has a small amount of halogen such as iodine or bromine added.

Heat Gain - Refers to the increase in temperature in a space, object, or structure that results from solar radiation. The amount of heat gain increases with the strength of the sun and varies with the ability of any intervening material to transmit or resist the radiation.

Holistic-design -An approach that emphasizes the functional relationship between the various building parts and the facility as a whole.

Instantaneous / On-demand Water Heater - A tankless water heater which heats by passing water through a coiled network of pipes with a gas burner or electric heating element.

Inverters - An apparatus that converts direct current (DC) into alternating current (AC), in this case in conjunction with a photovoltaic system. See also Micro-inverters.

Ipe - (pronounced "ee-pay") is a large tropical hardwood tree that grows abundantly throughout Central and South America. Ipe wood is prized for its durability, strength, and its natural resistance to decay, wet conditions, and insect infestation. Used for decks and countertops of the BeauSoleil Home.

Kilowatt (kW) - A measure of 1,000 watts of electrical power.

LED - A light-emitting diode is a semiconductor device that emits visible light when an electric current passes through it. The light is not particularly bright, but in most L.E.D.s it is monochromatic, occurring at a single wavelength.

LEED - The U.S. Green Building Council's sustainability rating system – Leadership in Environmental and Energy-Efficient Design.

Membrane - A selective barrier that allows the passage of certain constituents and retains other constituents found in the liquid usually used as waterproofing on the walls or roof of a building.

Micro-inverters - A solar micro-inverter converts direct current (DC) electricity from a single solar panel to alternating current (AC); the output from several micro-inverters is combined and often fed to the electrical grid. See also Inverters.

Mini-split System - Compact design split air conditioning or heat pump, available in a multitude of capacities, designs, styles, and simplified installation techniques, in this case wall-mounted without ductwork. Allows for multiple zones within a small home.

Modular - Employing or involving a module or modules as the basis of design or construction usually for portability and efficiency/speed of construction.

Murphy Bed - Also known as a wall bed, fold down bed, or pull down bed. It is a bed that is hinged at one end so it can be folded up and stored vertically against a wall or in a closet.

National Renewable Energy Laboratory (NREL) - The U.S. Department of Energy's primary national laboratory for renewable energy and energy efficiency research and development. NREL is the primary administrator of the Solar Decathlon.

Natural Ventilation - Ventilation provided by thermal, wind, or diffusion effects through doors, windows, and/or other intentional openings in the building. Natural ventilation systems may be either manually or automatically controlled. Convection (air movement from area of heat to colder area) and the venturi effect (a constricted opening reducing the pressure of air thus inducing suction) aid in the movement of air. Also called "suckulation," a term coined by Edward J. Cazayoux, FAIA.

Net-metering - A system in which solar panels or other renewable energy generators are connected to a public-utility power grid and surplus power is transferred onto the grid, allowing customers to offset the cost of power drawn from the utility.

Net-zero - A zero-energy building which produces as much energy as it consumes.

Off-Grid - Off-the-grid (OTG) can refer to living in a self-sufficient manner without reliance on one or more public utilities. Off-the-grid homes are autonomous; they do not rely on municipal water supply, sewer, natural gas, electrical power grid, or similar utility services.

Orientation / Location - The position of a house or building on its site, the disposition of the parts of a house or building with reference to the points of the compass.

Passive Design / Systems - Passive systems do not require electricity to operate. They operate under the natural principles of physics. Passive design is not an attachment or supplement to architectural design, but a design process that is integrated with architectural design.

Passive Daylighting - A system of both collecting sunlight using static, non-moving, and non-tracking systems (such as windows, sliding glass doors, most skylights or light tubes) and reflecting the collected daylight deeper inside with elements such as light shelves. Passive daylighting systems are different from active daylighting systems in that active systems track and/or follow the sun and rely on mechanical mechanisms to do so.

Passive Solar Heating - Passive strategies that can contribute to the heating and daylighting of nearly any building.

Permeable Paving - A range of cementitious and masonry materials with a gravel or sand base and subbase that allow the movement of stormwater through the surface. In addition to reducing runoff, this system effectively traps suspended solids and filters pollutants from the water.

Photovoltaic - The production of electric current at the junction of two substances exposed to light. Photons from sunlight cause electrons to be generated causing an electrical current.

Piers - A support system used in construction to elevate the superstructure above the ground plane or grade; the piers serve as columns for the superstructure and are typically concrete, masonry, or steel. See also CMU.

Plenum - An enclosed chamber, typically located under a home, for distribution of heated or conditioned air.

Precedent - A previous or existing building or structure that serves as an example for future building designs.

Program - The thorough and systematic evaluation of the interrelated values, goals, facts, and needs of a client's organization, facility users, and the surrounding community.

PV - See Photovoltaic

Rainwater Harvesting - The collection of water from surfaces on which rain falls and subsequent storing this water for later use. Normally water is collected from the roofs of buildings and stored in rainwater tanks. See also Cistern and Gutters and Downspouts

Rain-screen - The rain-screen is the siding itself but the term rain-screen also implies a system of building. Ideally the rain-screen prevents the wall air/moisture barrier on sheathing from getting wet. Often the system has an air-space behind it. See also Furring Strips

Raised Acadian Cottage - Side-gabled vernacular buildings of simple massing, normally having their front walls moved inward to make an integral porch under a single steep roofline; the form was originally brought to Louisiana by Acadian immigrants with a knowledge of long-span roof framing techniques.

Real-time Energy Dashboard - Showcases real-time building performance and green features and empowers occupants to become active participants in energy management. Real-time energy dashboard for the BeauSoleil Home: http://egauge1919.egaug.es/kiosk/

Roof Overhang - An eave or section of roof that extends past the plane of the vertical wall below.

Scheme - The documentation of written and graphic descriptions of the architectural elements of a building project, including sketches, drawings, and details to depict design solutions and strategies.

Shell - The building "envelope" is the physical separator between the conditioned and unconditioned environment of a building, including the resistance to air, water, heat, light, and noise transfer.

Shotgun House -A narrow rectangular domestic residence, usually no more than 12 feet wide, with rooms arranged one behind the other and doors at each end of the house

SIPs - Structural insulated panels are high performance building panels used as floors, walls, and roofs for residential and light commercial buildings. The panels are made by sandwiching a core of rigid foam plastic insulation between two structural facings, such as plywood.

SF - Square foot (plural square feet; abbreviated ft^2, sq. ft., or SF) is an imperial unit and U.S. customary unit (non-SI, non-metric) of area, used mainly in the United States, Canada, United Kingdom, Bangladesh, India, and Pakistan. It is defined as the area of a square with sides of 1 foot.

Smart Growth - Planned economic and community development that attempts to curb urban sprawl and worsening environmental conditions

Solar Panel System - The system is a combination of multiple solar panels that generate electricity, the inverter that transforms it into alternating current, and the installation materials such as mounting materials and cables. Could also refer to solar thermal panels. See also Flat-Plate Collector.

Solar Water Heater - A solar water heater uses the sun's energy to pre-heat household water before the conventional gas (or electric) water heater provides any additional required heating.

Studs - An upright support in the wall of a building to which sheathing, drywall, etc., are attached.

Sustainability - Seeks to minimize the negative environmental impact of buildings by efficiency and moderation in the use of materials, energy, and development. (Additional definitions: Shigeru Ban - "I hate waste." Kari Smith – "like a farm.")

Technological-hybrid - A hybrid energy system usually consists of two or more renewable energy sources used together to provide increased system efficiency as well as greater balance in energy supply.

Tectonics - The language of assembly and configuration of building components.

Translucent-polycarbonate / Polygal - Semi-transparent sheeting that are a virtually unbreakable glazing material manufactured from melted polymer resin. Materials are manufactured with a hollow-core structure, creating air spaces that act as insulation

Typologies - The classification of (usually physical) characteristics commonly found in buildings and urban places, according to their association with different categories, such as intensity of development (from natural or rural to highly urban), degrees of formality, and school of thought (for example, modernist or traditional). Individual characteristics form patterns. Patterns relate elements hierarchically across physical scales (from small details to large systems).

Vernacular - A category of architecture based on local needs and construction.

Watt (w) - The unit of power, equivalent to one joule per second, corresponding to the power in an electric circuit in which the potential difference is one volt and the current one ampere.

BIBLIOGRAPHY

"About Solar Decathlon." U.S. Department of Energy. Last updated April 4, 2014. http://www.solardecathlon.gov/about.html.

"About." URBANbuild. Tulane University, 2013. http://www.tulaneurbanbuild.com/index2.php#/rtext_2/1/.

Ancelet, Barry, J. Edwards, and G. Pitre. *Cajun Country*. Jackson, Miss.: University Press of Mississippi, 1991.

Architecture for Humanity, ed. *Design Like You Give a Damn: Architectural Responses to Humanitarian Crises*. New York: Metropolis Books, 2006.

Architecture for Humanity, ed. *Design like You Give a Damn. [2], Building Change from the Ground Up*. New York: Abrams, 2012.

"BeauSoleil Louisiana Solar Home Media Outreach Report." NHD. Undated.

"BeauSoleil Louisiana Solar Home Project Manual." Edited by W. Geoff Gjertson. Lafayette, La.: UL Lafayette, 2009. Also available online: http://www.solardecathlon.gov/past/2009/team_louisiana.html.

BeauSoleil Reunion Google Survey April 30, 2013. https://docs.google.com/forms/d/1oNAZ7wIFx8Grv1WG-t9Fnrr_e_tUf2zyclwfbLVJfKk/viewanalytics.

Benyus, Janine M. *Biomimicry: Innovation Inspired by Nature*. New York: Perennial, 2002.

"Bon Cher Camarade." 1980 radio program produced by Nick Spitzer for the National Public Radio series *Folk Festival USA*. Archive Collection #55-56, FT1201-1202. Southern Folklife Collection. Wilson Library, University of North Carolina.

Brasseaux, Carl A. *The Road to Louisiana: The Saint Domingue Refugees in Louisiana*. Edited by Glenn R. Conrad. Lafayette, La.: Center for Louisiana Studies, 1992.

Brearley, David. "Winning Ways: 2009 Solar Decathlon." *Home Power Magazine*. February/March 2010.

Brown, David E., Mindy Fox, and Mary Rickel Pelletier, eds. *Sustainable Architecture White Papers*. New York: Earth Pledge Foundation, 2000.

Brown, G. Z. *Sun, Wind, and Light: Architectural Design Strategies*. New York: Wiley, 2000.

Cazayoux, Edward Jon. "An Environmentally Responsive Residence for South Louisiana." Proceedings 8th National Passive Conference, American Solar Energy Soc. & DoE. (September 7-9, 1983): 873-87.

Cazayoux, Edward Jon. *A Manual for the Environmental & Climate Responsive Restoration and Renovation of Older Houses in Louisiana*. Baton Rouge, La.: Department of Natural Resources, 2003.

"Communication Success: UL Lafayette TEAM BeauSoleil 2009." Edited by John, Gjertson, Guidry, and Vanicor. Lafayette, La.: UL Lafayette, 2009.

Davidson, Joel and Fran Orner. *The New Solar Electric Home: The Complete Guide to Photovoltaics for Your Home*. Ann Arbor, Mich.: Aatec Publications, 2008.

Elliot, Stuart. "The Older Audience is Looking Better Than Ever." *New York Times*. April 20, 2009. National edition. http://www.nytimes.com/2009/04/20/business/20adcol.html.

Epstein, David. *The Sports Gene: Inside the Science of Extraordinary Athletic Performance*. New York: Penguin Group, 2013. As quoted on CBS Sunday Morning, April 6, 2014. http://www.cbsnews.com/news/are-elite-athletes-born-or-made/.

Frampton, K. "Towards a Critical Regionalism: Six Points for an Architecture of Resistance." Edited by H. Foster. *Postmodern Culture*. London: Pluto Press, 1983.

Fuller, Moore. *Environmental Control Systems: Heating Cooling Lighting*. New York: McGraw-Hill College, 1993.

Gjertson, W. Geoff. "A House Divided: Challenges for Design/Build Programs in Architecture Schools." Local Identities Global Challenges: 2011 ACSA Fall Conference, Houston. Edited by Sabouni, Ikhlas, and Jorge Vanegas. (2012): 23-35.

Gore, Al. *An Inconvenient Truth*. New York: Rodale, 2006.

Kieran, Stephen and James Timberlake. *Refabricating Architecture: How Manufacturing Methodologies are Poised to Transform Building Construction*. New York: McGraw-Hill Professional, 2003.

Kormann, Carolyn. "Shigeru Ban: Shelter From The Storm." *The New Yorker*. October 2, 2011. http://www.newyorker.com/online/blogs/festival/2011/10/shigeru-ban-shelter-from-the-storm.html .

Kwok, Alison G. *The Green Studio Handbook: Environmental Strategies for Schematic Design*. Burlington, Mass.: Architectural Press, 2007.

LaSala, Hector. "The Building Institute: A Civic-Engagement Instrument." *New York Times*. August 9, 2006. http://www.nytimes.com/2006/08/09/college/collegespecial2/coll-adp-building.html?pagewanted=print&action=click&module=Search&region=searchResults&mabReward=relbias%3Ar&url=http%3A%2F%2Fquery.nytimes.com%2Fsearch%2Fsitesearch%2F%23%2Fhector%2Blasala%2Bbuilding%2Binstitute%2F&_r=0.

Lavelle, Marianne. "For Hurricane Katrina Victims, A Solar Restart." *National Geographic*. August 2010. http://news.nationalgeographic.com/news/2010/08/100826-katrina-green-buildings-solar-energy/.

"Leadership in Energy & Environmental Design (LEED)." U.S. Green Building Council. Last modified 2014. http://www.usgbc.org/leed?gclid=COa82_Twx74CFeJF7AodQw4AoA.

Lentz, Timothy Roberts. "Analysis of the passive design and solar collection techniques of the houses in the 2009 U.S. Department of Energy's Solar Decathlon competition." Ames: Iowa State University, 2010.

Mandell, Julia. "Up to Speed." *Metropolis Online Magazine*. May 2006. http://www.metropolismag.com/May-2006/Up-to-Speed/.

"Mission." University of Louisiana at Lafayette. Accessed May 25, 2014. http://www.louisiana.edu/about-us/who-we-are/mission-vision-values.

Mockbee, Samuel. "About Samuel 'Sambo' Mockbee." 2009-2014. http://samuelmockbee.net/biography/.

McDonough, William. *Cradle to Cradle: Remaking the Way We Make Things*. New York: North Point Press, 2002.

Pierce, Deborah. *The Accessible Home: Designing for All Ages and Abilities*. Newtown, Conn.: Taunton, 2012.

Pulkka, Wesley. "Antoine Predock: architecture and time." Trendmagazineglobal.com, Fall 2009/Winter 2010, 63.

Rahim, Saquib. "The Quest to Build an "Ethically Responsible House." *New York Times*. October 9, 2009. Last updated 2009. http://www.nytimes.com/cwire/2009/10/09/09climatewire-the-quest-to-build-an-ethically-responsible-12926.html?pagewanted=all.

Sammons, Thomas, ed. "Waterfront Development: Delcambre, Louisiana." Community Design Workshop, UL Lafayette. Delcambre Master Plan. PDF found on Louisiana Sea Grant website: www.laseagrant.org. Last updated on May 12, 2014. http:// www.laseagrant.org/pdfs/delcambre_ulldesignworkshop.pdf.

Sawyers, Harry. "14 Best New Technologies For Greener Homes." *Popular Mechanics*. April 2010. http://www.popularmechanics.com/home/improvement/energy-efficient/4350127.

Solar Decathlon Proposal 2009. Edited by W. Geoff Gjertson. Lafayette, La.: UL Lafayette, 2007.

Spell, Sarah. "Power House." *La Louisiane*. Spring 2009, 21.

"Studio 804 Mission." University of Kansas, Architecture, Design and Planning. http://studio804.com/.

TEAM BeauSoleil Blog. http://believeinbeausoleil.blogspot.com/.
"The dbX: What is it?," Edited by Christopher Trumble. Last updated April 14, 2014. http://www.db-x.org/.
Vinnitskaya, Irina. "The Zachary House / Stephen Atkinson Architecture." *ArchDaily*. October 20, 2012. Accessed May 25, 2014. http://www.archdaily.com/282552/the-zachary-house-stephen-atkinson-architecture/.
"Welcome Home. Bienvenue a la maison: Believe in tomorrow, Beginning today." Last updated 2011. http://www.beausoleilhome.org/content/home/index_2.html.
Williams, Austin. "Rainscreen cladding: letting air in to keep rain out." NBS Shortcuts, the nbs.com. http://www.thenbs.com/topics/DesignSpecification/articles/rainscreenCladding.asp.
Zehner, Ozzie. *Green Illusions: The Dirty Secrets of Clean Energy and the Future of Environmentalism*. Lincoln: University of Nebraska Press, 2012.

ILLUSTRATION/ PHOTO CREDITS

Atkinson Architecture
page 51 top

Megan Barra
page 43, 62

Allison Bohl DeHart
page 71

Garrett Armentor
sidebars: page 47, 50, 54, 60, 80, 84, 89, 92, 93, 94, 100

Building Institute
page 138, 160

Jeffrey K. Bounds
page 40

David Carroll
page 115

Edward Cazayoux
page 15, 16, 25 bottom right, 45 top, 54, 90 top

CMPBS
page 11 top

CMPBS/UT School of Architecture
page 12 bottom

Scott Chappuis
page 23, 131, 143, 149

Denny Culbert
page 140 right, 142 top

Robert Dafford
page 42 top

Tim Dumatrait
page 52

Chelsea Ellison
page 29, 34, 37, 57, 67 top and bottom, 86, 140 left and middle

Lucius Fontenot
page 31

Fleming Artists
page 42 bottom

Kerry Frey
page 87 top and middle, 88 bottom

Philip Gould
front cover, page 7, 19, 24, 26, 41, 49, 64, 68, 78, 79 top, 81 top, 82, 84, 85 top and middle, 88 top, 89 top, 90 bottom, 94, 95, 96 top, 97, 98, 99, 100, 101, 106, 108, 109, 111, 112, 114 top, 116 bottom, 118, 119, 120 top, 121, 122 top, 123-128, 132

W. Geoff Gjertson
page 36, 53 bottom, 66, 72 top. 77 top, 83 top, 89 bottom, 92, 107, 116 top

Catherine Guidry
page 53 top right, 56, 91, 93, 96 lower, 110, 120 middle and bottom

Habitat For Humanity International
page 38 left and middle

Robin Hebert-Guidry
page 25 bottom left

Mimi Kwan/CMPBS/ UT School of Architecture
page 13 middle

Chris Leger
page 80

Rich MacMath/CMPBS
page 11 bottom

Benjamin Magallon
page 136

Robin May
page 139 top, 141 top

Michael McClure
page 38 right

Elemore Morgan Jr.
page 39, 48

Kit Morris
page 12 top

Chris O'Connor
page 46

Prakash Patel
page 9, 13 top and bottom, 30

Brian C. Miller Richard
page 67 middle

RUSSO
page 62, 74

Haylei Smith
139 middle and bottom, 141 middle and bottom, 142 bottom

TEAM Beausoleil
title page, page 45 bottom, 47, 48 top, 51 bottom, 53 middle, 55, 58, 72 bottom, 77 bottom, 79 bottom, 81 bottom, 83 bottom, 85 bottom, 87 bottom

UL Lafayette
page 73, 76

Stefano Paltera/US Department of Energy
backcover, page 25 top, 63, 102, 103, 113, 114 bottom, 117, 122 bottom

US Navy
Page 105

INDEX